"Women today are inundated by confusing messages about who they ought to be. *The New Eve* goes straight to the heart of who they were created to be. Robert Lewis does a masterful job of weaving challenges, stories, and biblical truths together. This book will help women gain insights into making their unique lives better, richer, and more meaningful in a way that glorifies God."

Gayle Carpenter
Chief Administrative Officer
Leadership Network

"Robert Lewis sounds a much-needed message as he calls women to walk in the feminine freedom and fullness that result from embracing our core biblical callings. *The New Eve* dispels the current cultural fog regarding what it means to be a woman by looking to God's design, as revealed in the Scripture, for wisdom, insight, and direction."

Nancy Leigh DeMoss
Author and
Host of *Revive Our Hearts* radio

"Women today have unprecedented opportunities and possibilities before them, but this great new freedom also brings a new dilemma: how to make the best choices for their own good and that of their families. In *The New Eve,* Robert Lewis gives women of all ages a picture of what God intended for us from the beginning and a clear vision for how we make choices that liberate us to live with purposeful direction. No matter your stage in life, all women can benefit from his coaching. Having known Robert and his wife Sherard since college, I can confidently say this is not just great material. It is a reflection of two godly people who are always working to live marriage and family as God intended. I highly recommend it and hope it will be widely read."

Barbara Rainey
FamilyLife Cofounder
and Author

THE NEW
eve

THE NEW
eve

CHOOSING **GOD'S BEST** FOR YOUR LIFE

Foreword by
SHAUNTI FELDHAHN | **ROBERT LEWIS**
with Jeremy Howard

B&H
PUBLISHING GROUP
NASHVILLE, TENNESSEE

ISBN: 978-0-8054-4687-6

Published by B&H Publishing Group
Nashville, Tennessee

Dewey Decimal Classification: 248.843
Subject Heading: CHRISTIAN LIFE \ WOMEN

Scripture taken from the New American Standard Bible®,
Copyright © 1960, 1962, 1963, 1968, 1971, 1972, 1973, 1975, 1977,
1995 by The Lockman Foundation. Used by permission.

1 2 3 4 5 6 7 8 9 10 11 12 13 14 15   12 11 10 09 08

To women everywhere
who are bold enough
to trust Jesus Christ
with their lives and their priorities.

Eternity belongs to you.

Contents

Foreword

I never thought a book written by a man could give me such an eye-opening picture of who I should be as a woman—or that it would have such a big impact on my life.

It will impact your life, too . . . if you let it.

It's All about How We Are Designed

Many of you might be familiar with Robert Lewis' organization, Men's Fraternity, that has somehow attracted hundreds of thousands of bleary-eyed men into early-morning video Bible studies across the country. While we might have thought men just wanted to have their own version of a good Beth Moore talking-to, there was something much deeper attracting these guys. Robert was giving them a vision, a model for what it means to be a godly, biblically-guided man in a culture that no longer agrees on what that ideal looks like—or whether it's even necessary. A model that men could measure their personal and professional life by . . . and a challenge to change it if it didn't measure up.

Well, ladies, it's our turn. Many of us try to live a godly life and follow the Bible's specific precepts. But without ever intending to, we could still be fighting against how God has designed us—simply because the world of women looks so very different from the way it did in biblical times and we haven't had a modern-day model to go by.

This is not just an academic issue. We have professional and personal choices that were unheard of for women two thousand years ago; but God has still designed us as women in a specific way, and that design affects everything in our lives, whether we like it or not. Reading this book, I finally realized: I can commit my daily life and my eternal future to Christ, and I can try to follow the Bible's directives as best I can—but my most important choices could still be at odds with how God has designed me! And if that's the case, I will have regret instead of contentment. What's more, I will drastically limit my ability to be a good steward of the gifts God has given me.

Whether you are a stay-at-home mom or an airplane-hopping executive, a student or a senior adult, this book will give you a modern, encouraging vision for what it means to be a godly, biblically guided woman in the twenty-first century. In an era where women rightfully have high expectations personally and professionally, and *can* do almost anything we set our minds to, this model will help us navigate what we *should* do—and should not do.

Some Very Personal Encouragement

I know this has profoundly helped me. As some of you might guess, I'm extremely busy both professionally and personally. I'm a best-selling author, columnist, and traveling speaker; but I'm also a wife and a mom to two young children. I try to be a supportive wife to my husband's entrepreneurial business, but I also have my own.

And privately, for years, I have been torn by how to balance it all; how to keep all the plates spinning. With *The New Eve,* I finally feel like I have a clear and realistic model that I can look up to and respect as a modern Christian woman; something that can help me make the decisions that will lead to relief, delight, and fulfillment instead of regret.

That doesn't mean those decisions are easy. For me, it has meant a willingness to reexamine some professional opportunities in light of personal ones. For others, it may mean examining whether you are fully utilizing your unique God-given gifts for the impact He intends you to have. But once you make these decisions, they will *fit.* You—like me—will feel like you're finally functioning in the way you were designed for. The specific answers will be wonderfully individual for every wonderfully individual woman, but the vision of womanhood is the same.

Be willing to be challenged, sisters. The end result will be worth it.

—Shaunti Feldhahn

Acknowledgments

Two are better than one," the Scripture says, "because they have a good return for their labor" (Eccles. 4:9). I've found this to be true in my writing, and *The New Eve* is certainly no exception. Each book is clearly "better" because of the help given by a number of very talented and supportive people.

First and foremost on this list is Jeremy Howard. Shortly after finishing his Ph.D. program, Jeremy made a courageous move to Little Rock to assist me in a number of writing projects. I can honestly say that without Jeremy's energetic spirit, superb professionalism, and writing partnership, *The New Eve* would have never found its way into print. Thanks, Jeremy, for all your hard work and the positive attitude in which you did it. It has been a privilege working with you. My best to you and Simone and your family as you now embark on a new writing adventure.

I owe a huge debt of gratitude as well to a number of special women—Gayle Carpenter, Deborah Harris, Cheryl Rainy, Virginia Robinson, and Linda Slaton—who took the time to read my ever-evolving manuscript and offer their insightful comments and helpful suggestions. Ladies, please know that your input made this book better in a number of significant ways. A special thanks to my wonderful daughters, Rebekah Lewis and

Elizabeth James, for the hours they put in reading and re-reading specific chapters and talking out with me various ideas and concepts. You both made a real difference. I would also like to say a special thank-you to Shaunti Feldhahn for going the extra mile and giving me her in-depth analysis of the manuscript. What a much needed assist that was!

Much of the artwork you find in *The New Eve* came from the creative mind of Nancy Carter. Nancy has helped me with graphics on a number of my books through the years and always does so with a bright smile and a servant's heart. Thanks *again*, Nancy.

I also want to thank Lisa Fischer for being willing to carve out time for me in her busy schedule to serve as my host for the Discussion Starter DVD that was produced to support New Eve discussion groups and the study guide found in the back of the book. (This DVD is available at www.mensfraternity.com.) You did a great job, Lisa, and you made it fun too.

Speaking of video, Jud Archer and his crew—Steve Childress, Thomas Rogers, Claes Jonasson, James Groves, Nancy Shepard, and Dave Calhoun—deserve a special high five for the great work they did in filming and editing. Jud, it was like old times being with you again in the editing suite.

Dr. Margaret Feurtado graciously took the lead in holding this project up in prayer, and how grateful and blessed I was that she did! Thank you, Margaret.

Ruthie George also deserves a special mention. It was Ruthie who first urged me to speak on this subject and later gave me the opportunity to do so while she served as the Women's Ministry Director of our church. Ruthie, I hope you like what you started.

Thanks to Helen Carter, my administrative assistant, for all the support she gave Jeremy and me during the long days of this writing project. Each day we were greeted with a big, bright "GOOD MORNING!"

Then there is the publishing team at B&H, beginning with David R. Shepherd and Leonard G. Goss, who head the editorial squad. Lisa Parnell was the project manager for this book, Diana Lawrence oversaw the cover design, and David Chandler was responsible for physical production of the book and the DVD. Thank you all for believing in this project and making it come to life. It's been a pleasure working with you.

Finally, to my wife Sherard, it's hard to know what to say because whatever it would be, it wouldn't be enough. You are priceless . . . and always have been!

It really is true, "Two—and many more—are better than one."

Preface

Iknow what you're thinking. It's the obvious question. *What's a man doing writing a book for women?* Personally, I've asked myself that same question many times over the past year as I've compiled this manuscript. On the occasions when I've had the opportunity to talk with my male friends about this project, they've engaged me with a look that says, "He could be losing it."

So why did I write this book? Here's the answer: because women strongly encouraged me to do so. Believe me, this book would have never found its way into print if a chorus of feminine voices had not urged me to go forward and do it.

Of course, there's a story that goes with that. For nearly two decades I have enjoyed a wonderfully fulfilling ministry called Men's Fraternity. I started this with thirty men who met with me weekly to explore core issues and concerns men deal with every day in their hearts and lives. It is real-life stuff men quickly connect with. God obviously blessed it, because soon more than a thousand men were joining me each week for this journey. Best of all, I saw significant levels of positive and powerful change in the lives of many of the men who participated—so much so that their girlfriends or wives began to buzz about the good things they were observing in their men. Many of these women actually began to listen to tapes of my weekly Men's Fraternity presentations. No doubt they were curious as to what was really going on. Evidently they liked what they heard, because it wasn't long until I was approached by some of the women leaders in our church with the idea of doing something similar with the women. For several years I only laughed and said, "No way. I'm not a woman."

Then four years ago I was approached again with a more limited invitation: would I address key biblical principles for helping women better construct and manage their lives in a way that honors God and avoids unnecessary sorrows in the whirl of the modern world? To me, that felt much more appropriate and doable. It was within the scope of my competency, so I agreed to do it.

I gave my first set of "New Eve" lectures to some three hundred women in Little Rock in 2004. Then, a short time later, I did it again before six hundred women in Rockford, Illinois, just outside Chicago. Both groups gave me very positive feedback. In fact, a number of the women who attended these sessions have since gone on and used the CDs and DVDs that were produced from these conferences to conduct New Eve study and discussion groups of their own. Meanwhile, many women began to ask me if I would consider redrafting this material into a book. After a time of weighing the risks and seeking God's direction on this possibility, I decided to move forward.

So here we are.

My sincere hope is that in reading this book, you will find the same kind of eye-opening encouragement other women have told me they've received through hearing my New Eve talks. Let me assure you that what you find here will not be a one-size-fits-all, cookie-cutter approach to womanhood supported by Bible verses. This is not about becoming a biblical Barbie or recapturing a 1950s model of womanhood; nor is it about promising a formula for a trouble-free life. Life can get messy even when you make the right choices, as many of you know. Thus, my approach is simply to offer hands-on, proven guidelines for making your unique life better, richer, and more meaningful. I've seen the benefit of these guidelines in the lives of my adult daughters as they have navigated the highs and lows of their professional careers and personal lives.

Therefore, I have built the New Eve around five big-picture faith strategies. I call these strategies *bold moves* because living them out requires bold faith. They serve as guardrails for a woman's life, not only protecting her from harm but also leading her to a more satisfying, purposeful, and God-honoring lifestyle. But courageous faith is required to embrace them.

Finally, let me say a word about the title, *The New Eve*. You're probably wondering why I chose that title. I did so for two reasons. First, the Eve story in Genesis is a gold mine of helpful feminine insight, extremely useful in constructing a lifestyle that works for today's modern woman. Second, Eve is much more than merely the first woman. She powerfully represents a *type* of woman. Amid the immense freedoms and opportunities of the garden God had placed her in, Eve made bad choices that squandered her potential and unleashed a painful life of regret.

The term *New Eve* therefore becomes a metaphor for a second type of woman who counters the first Eve. She is a woman of keen discernment. She is a woman who has learned how to navigate our modern world and its endless opportunities—some of which are forbidden fruit—and make right choices. That's because she is a woman whose biblical convictions run deep. And her choices bring her precisely the opposite of what the first Eve experienced. Rather than pain and regret, the New Eve finds that her bold moves have unleashed a growing sense of satisfaction and freedom into her life.

Every woman is an Eve. You'll see that clearly in the pages ahead. All that's really in question is: Which type of Eve will you be? Will your life look more like the foolish original or the new one who makes better choices? I truly believe the five bold moves I set forth here can go a long way in helping you find the more rewarding path.

If at this point I have stirred your interest and answered your questions, then let me encourage you to join me on this New Eve journey.

1

I Am Woman

Anita woke up at 6:00 a.m. Normally she would lie in bed and think, pray, and plan until Ron awoke, but not today. For weeks, *months*, this day had crowded everything else out of her mind. But enough with thinking. It was time to move.

After a quick shower she dressed and headed for the kitchen. She paused to peek inside her children's rooms. Empty. A sense of loss streaked across her heart. When the kids were young, she had negotiated a part-time employment arrangement with her boss in order to be with them. Motherhood then had been about monsters under the bed, scraped knees, Big Wheels, bedtime stories, and the never-ending question: "Why, Mommy?" Later it became endless carpools, schoolwork, athletic events, and volatile boy-girl relationships. Anita had been there for it all, having put a great career track on hold to be at home. She'd do it all again in a heartbeat. There were no regrets except that this time had passed. The kids were in college now, and she had reengaged her career full time five years ago.

As Anita set the coffeemaker in motion, the business of the day rushed back upon her. She smiled at the tension in her stomach, then turned on the TV at the breakfast bar to catch news about her sister. Select polls had been open for more than an hour now; newscasters were poring over anemic streams of data, somehow converting them into "scientific" predictions on how the day would unfold. "Joanna Taylor is sure to win the Senate seat," said one pollster. "No, no, this thing is still up for grabs," countered another. Anita tried not to listen, but she couldn't think of not listening. "Go, Sis, go!" she breathed.

"How's she doing?" Ron asked as he came into the kitchen.

"Far too early to say," Anita replied. "It's silly of me to be watching."

"Not at all," Ron said as he drew up next to her and gave a reassuring hug.

"I've got to get going," Anita said, quickly refocusing on the day's big events. "I'll swing by the poll and vote, *several times* if I can," she laughed. "Then I'm meeting Sandy at 10:00 for a final walk-through of the merger contract before I report for jury duty."

Ron shook his head in admiration. "You're something, you know that? Today your sister's set to become a U.S. senator, you're closing one of the biggest deals your company has ever made, and still you don't bother to ask for exemption from jury duty. What else can you fit into this day? Hey, the driveway needs resealing," he suggested with a wry smile.

Anita laughed as she finished off a muffin. "Mostly I just want Sis to get that Senate seat! The other stuff is secondary."

"Just be home in time for us to enjoy this night together, OK?" Ron said.

"You got it," Anita answered firmly. Then, with a sigh of reflection, she paused and said, "Ron, think about what this day means." A photograph, framed in red, sat atop the counter in front of her. She turned it so Ron could see. It was Anita's great-grandmother. "Grandma Parry never saw a day like this. She was smart and ambitious, but she never set foot in a college. She never held a job that paid real money either, let alone run for an elected office. Yet in many ways all the opportunities that are given to Sis and me are owed to her and others like her. That two big moments for Sis and me happen to fall on the same day is perhaps God's special way of reminding us of how privileged we are."

Ron nodded. "Well, by tonight I'll have a senator in the family and a savvy businesswoman who knows her way around a jury box. Great day to be a Parry woman!"

"A great day to be a *woman*," Anita corrected him. She righted the picture frame, blew Ron a kiss, and stepped out into a world of opportunity that her great-grandmother could never have imagined.

Unlimited Opportunity

It *is* a great day to be a woman. The opportunities now available to you and women everywhere in the twenty-first century are astounding. You have more power—personally, professionally, and politically—than at any other time in human history. And that power trajectory is predicted to rise even further in the decades to come. "Women will rock," predicts Ron Fournier, author of *Applebee's America*. Today they "are getting better grades, running a majority of student governments, and graduating from college in larger numbers than their male counterparts." In the future "the best and the brightest will be women."[1]

Celinda Lake and Kellyanne Conway foresee an even bolder outlook for women through their research. They write, "Without fanfare, almost stealthily, America has become women-centric. . . . Women—from seniors to boomers to Generations X and Y—are recasting the nation in their image" and "shaking the culture to its core."[2]

These statements are especially breathtaking when one remembers how far women have come in such a very short time. Fewer than one hundred years ago, *you couldn't even vote as a woman!* Opportunities, as compared to men's, were extremely limited. For the most part, a woman's world was defined primarily by husband and home.

But then new winds began to blow. Changes in the law expanded a woman's horizons. Women won the right to vote (by *one vote*) in 1920 and with it gained a new voice and powerful influence in shaping society. Growing educational opportunities opened up a woman's mind to new possibilities. The advent of World War II gave thousands of women new experiences. Many discovered they could do "a man's job" by working in factories and running assembly lines, building and flying airplanes, managing businesses, and constructing the war machine their men unleashed half a world away.

After the war, technology opened up a woman's time. Chores that once took hours were now finished with the touch of a button. A woman's schedule was now freer than ever before for "something more." But what?

Finally, the feminist movement of the '70s and '80s opened up a woman's fighting spirit. She no longer had to stay quiet, stay at home, or stay married. Where society refused to change to accommodate her, she herself confronted and fought to change it. "I am woman, hear me roar!" Helen Reddy sang as newly liberated women broke into male-dominated domains, overturned rigid social structures, and took new ground for their ever-growing ambitions. Today that "roar" is louder than ever.

Now in the twenty-first century, women like you have more rights, choices, and freedoms than ever before. In many areas, women have not only achieved equality with men but have also *surpassed* their male counterparts. For example:

Workforce. Half of the American workforce is female. From 1976 to 1999 the percentage of American women who were working soared from 57 percent to 77 percent.[3]

Equal Pay . . . Greater Pay. A third of working wives outearn their working husbands.[4] This percentage is expected to rise significantly in the next decade.

Business Ownership. Nearly half of all American businesses are at least 50 percent owned by women. These firms, small and large, employ 19.1 million people and generate $2.5 trillion in annual revenue.[5]

Business Management. By 2001 women held close to 50 percent of all high-paying managerial, executive, and administrative jobs. As of 2004, 15 percent of Fortune 500 companies had a female CEO, a 20 percent increase since 2002. Top companies are increasingly topped by women![6]

Church Involvement and Lay Leadership. After a nationwide survey, George Barna concluded that "women shoulder most of the responsibility for the health and vitality of the Christian faith in the United States."[7]

Education. From kindergarten to graduate school, females are achieving far more than males; so much so that one leading publication says males are now the "second sex."[8]

College Enrollment. Women outnumber men by 30 percent in American colleges. That adds up to two million more women attending college than men. That's a stunning turnaround from the 1960s, when 66 percent of college students were men. Furthermore, female students are 33 percent more likely to graduate than their male counterparts.[9] The *New York Times* summed it up this way in a front-page headline: "At Colleges, Women Are Leaving Men in the Dust." The *Times* went on to say, "Academically, boys are about where they were 30 years ago, but girls are just on a tear, doing much, much better."[10]

Bachelor's Degrees. In fields of study ranging from biology to business, history to social science, and psychology to education, women are earning the majority of bachelor's degrees.[11] How many more? At least 200,000 more bachelor's degrees are awarded to women than men, according to the National Center of Education Statistics.[12]

Master's Degrees. Women now earn more than 50 percent of all master's degrees.[13]

MBA Enrollment. Women now compose 35 percent of all students in MBA programs.[14] In some business schools that percentage is much higher. For instance, at the Whittemore School of Business, one of the top one hundred graduate business schools in the nation, 61 percent of its full-time students are now women. That's up from 29 percent in 2004.[15]

Medical School. By 2003–2004 females composed 48 percent of all medical students, up from only 6 percent in 1960.[16] This percentage is expected to grow.

Law School. Women make up 50 percent of all new law students.[17]

All of these statistics are revealing, but the ones concerning education are especially telling because education is the best predictor of future demographics. As U.S. Secretary of Education Margaret Spellings says, the predominance of women on college campuses "has profound implications for the economy, society, families, and democracy."[18] All indications are that women will gain a clear majority in most professional fields as the twenty-first century progresses. As this enormous social realignment continues to play out, men will increasingly find themselves working for and tailoring their lives to women rather than vice versa. Whether men and women will adapt well to this new arrangement remains to be seen, but it is coming. The spotlight is clearly on the rising power of women.

A Warning from History

While it's true that freedom, power, and opportunity are wonderful assets to a woman's portfolio, there is a dark side. History illustrates this by pointing us back to other occasions when women had far-reaching rights and freedoms at their fingertips. In his book *Caesar and Christ*, Will Durant detailed one prime example of this from the first two centuries AD, when women in the major urban centers of the Roman Empire experienced their own season of liberation. Indeed, the parallels to our present day make Rome feel like America's historical twin.

That's because Roman women of this era had also acquired new and expanded freedoms that went well beyond the traditional boundaries. Long held back by law and custom, they won unprecedented rights for themselves and a level playing field with men. With this new power, they became doctors and lawyers, owned property, and traded goods. They enjoyed the liberty of conducting business with men in private quarters. This new tang of freedom was exhilarating, dizzying, and seductive.

Wisdom and restraint soon became the enemies of this newfound freedom rather than guardrails for it. Excess and foolishness disguised as chic became the new virtues. Women threw off modesty and walked the streets wearing however little they liked. Adulteries increased so much as to deaden the sense of scandal. Divorce was common; open marriage more so. Men preferred concubines to wives, and wives sought lovers in full view of their husbands. Abortion became a mundane means of birth control. Women lobbied for and eventually won the right to fight alongside men in military combat roles.

Classic femininity became decidedly out of vogue in the new Rome. With this new femininity and the shift from an agrarian to a cosmopolitan social structure, women pursued new, more aggressive roles in society and, along with their husbands, gave less and less attention to their homes.

Does any of this sound familiar?

Predictably, family problems exploded and birthrates fell sharply. Childbearing interrupted opportunity and the pursuit of beauty, so women avoided it like the plague. Caesar Augustus was so alarmed at these developments that he moved to bolster the image of motherhood in Rome by according mothers special honor in public. He dressed them in fine robes, exempted them from taxes, seated them in the luxury boxes at the Colosseum, and in earnest bid the nation do homage to the institute of motherhood. But his bid failed. The new Roman woman simply wasn't interested.[19]

In a final reflection on Rome's gender revolution, Durant noted that these women in their liberty chose more often than not to emulate men's *vices* rather than their virtues. Perhaps more to the point, Roman women took their new equality with men as an opportunity to become virtually indistinguishable from the men they once chafed under and disdained.[20] Some feminists of our own era have noted this same tendency among modern women. French activist Simone de Beauvoir, for instance, concluded, "It's quite obvious that once they are in power, women are exactly like men."[21]

I believe the freedoms and opportunities women like yourself have gained in this past century are wonderful assets. Everything is in place for you to excel. However, history shows that the freedom to excel also brings with it the freedom to bind yourself to greater evils and new sorrows.

What's a Woman to Choose?

Freedom always comes with forbidden fruit.

Many modern women already know this reality firsthand. Many others—maybe you—are starting to feel the tension that comes with unlimited freedom and opportunity. Gone are the days where there was one prescribed path for women to follow. Now there are endless options and lifestyles from which to choose—some good, some bad, some disastrous, but each promising the same thing on the front end: *life.*

So how do you discover what's best for you? Where is the help that can cut through the fog (especially for young women) to help you decide how to live smart and well? Unfortunately, today there is a lack of "life coaching" (the kind mentioned in Titus 2) that offers trustworthy navigational guidelines to assist women in discerning which choices are best and which, however alluring, might be empty promises or tragic dead ends. All of this leaves women asking, "How do I know on the front end which choices deliver the most out of life? And how do I avoid major mistakes and lifelong disappointments?" Such are the questions constantly circling around today's woman.

What adds additional anxiety is knowing that any choice you make *for* something is also a choice to *miss out* on something else. As Caitlin Flanagan said, "The unpleasant truth [is] that life presents a series of choices, each of which precludes a host of other attractive possibilities."[22] Without some kind of assurance, the haunting questions within each life choice are these: "Did I do the right thing? Was this the best for me, or did I miss the best?"

Looking back on their lives, many women wonder, *What was I thinking?* For instance, choosing to participate in the sexual revolution seemed liberating to many women years ago. But now that the kids have come and many dads have gone (nearly 40 percent of all children growing up today are fatherless; 50 percent of children born to mothers ages eighteen to twenty-four are without dads) and now that STDs and AIDS have come and stayed, how liberating was it? What about the hidden abortion or the sexual flashbacks? Liberating or enslaving? Is this the direction you want to offer your daughter or a younger woman as the way to a fulfilling life? Surely not. And yet everywhere—in movies, in music, and public role models—this forbidden fruit is still being advocated and glamorized as part of a new and improved womanhood. Many of today's young women are quick to take the bite.

Recently, a major advertising agency polled five hundred men and five hundred women, asking them at what point in a relationship they thought it was OK to have sex. The majority of men said on the fourth or fifth date. The women said between the first and second.[23]

Many women also continue to buy into one of the oldest pickup lines in the book: "You can have it all!" Like their great-ancestor Eve, they embrace this forbidden idea (Gen. 3:3–4) with passion, believing they can have everything without missing anything. They soon discover that this seductive promise is nothing more than the big, painful lie it has always been. This is especially true in the very sensitive subject of children and career. Can you have both? Of course. Can you do both well? That depends on a host of factors—your use of wisdom and an honest accounting of your limitations being chief among them. But you can't have it all in the absolute sense. Something or someone always gets left out or deeply hurt when you try.

Maria Shriver, a celebrated TV commentator and the wife of California Governor Arnold Schwarzenegger, has learned this hard truth. In her book *Ten Things I Wish I'd Known—Before I*

Went Out into the Real World, she offers the following advice: "You can't have an exciting, successful, powerful career and at the same time win the mother-of-the-year award and be wife and lover extraordinaire. No one can. If you see successful, glamorous women on magazine covers proclaiming they do it all, believe me, you're not getting the whole story." She then admitted, "Once you have children, you not only can't do it all, you can't do it the same way you were doing it before. In other words, once you start a family, don't expect to be the same hard-driving, workaholic, do-anything, go-anywhere worker you were. Because if you are, your children will suffer."[24]

Meredith Vieira, a former host of *The View* and now a co-anchor of NBC's *Today* show, gave an insightful interview to *Time* magazine's Jeff Chu. Chu asked, "You quit *60 Minutes* to focus on your family, but you now seem to juggle motherhood and work well. What do you say to women who want to have it all?" Vieira replied, "I hate that expression. When I left *60 Minutes*, I had women who came up to me very angry and said, 'You know, you were proof you could have it all. How dare you leave?' I thought that was ridiculous—I would lie to myself to create a lie for everybody else? You have to prioritize. If you can fit in job and kids and be comfortable with it, great. At that point, I realized I couldn't do it and give my kids and husband what they needed."[25]

My question is, Who's teaching young women that they can't have it all? The truth is, virtually no one. And when someone like Shriver or Vieira ventures out to admit that having it all is a myth, she is usually skewered and quickly dispensed with by so-called progressives who hold that "having it all" is the Holy Grail for women.

Of course, you can escape this difficult balancing act by simply eliminating children from the equation altogether. Young women are increasingly choosing this option as they see female icons like Oprah and Rachael Ray lead by example. In an interview with *Good Housekeeping* magazine, Ray, the megastar of Food Network, admitted that the demands on her time meant that motherhood would not likely find a spot on her calendar anytime soon. Said Ray, "Now I'm in my late 30's, and I've committed to so much work in the next three years that I think it would be really selfish to attempt to have a child."[26]

Selfish to have a child? Or could it be that this new womanhood is so "into self" that there is no room for loving children? This me-first attitude is part of the new fruit offered to young, modern Eves. It is glamorous and appealing. But before reaching for this fruit, you would do well to heed the words of Sylvia Ann Hewlett. When she set out to interview scores of highly successful women who were well into their careers, she assumed she would hear stories of celebrity status, power, and money that made children an easy trade-off. But "this is *not* what these women said. Rather, they told haunting stories of children being crowded out of their lives by high-maintenance careers and needy partners.... I was taken aback by what I heard. Going into these interviews I had assumed that if these accomplished, powerful women were childless, surely they had chosen to be. I was absolutely prepared to understand that the exhilaration and challenge of a megawatt career made it easy to decide not to be a mother. Nothing could be further from the truth. When I talked to these women about children, their sense of loss was palpable. I could see it in their faces, hear it in their voices, and sense it in their words."[27]

There you have it. Some of America's most successful women confess that the thrill of climbing to the top is not so fulfilling when they leave behind some of their greatest feminine callings to get there. But it will take much more than an occasional confessional from successful businesswomen to correct the course many women are on today. What is needed is a multitude of wise mentors. Some women are already doing this, but we need more.

I believe younger women would love for older, life-smart women to step forward and courageously speak into the confusion and empty rhetoric of much of today's modern femininity and offer rock-solid ways to build a life. They yearn for the life coaches I mentioned earlier—women who can point them to a life that is not only sensible and satisfying (Titus 2:5) but one that can go the distance without pulling up somewhere lame with regret. So where are the voices of this wisdom?

The truth is, when younger women look to their older contemporaries, they get more questions than answers. News anchor Alison Stewart illustrates the surprise and even disappointment many young women feel when they see deep tensions in older career women who look backward on their choices. She said, "When my friends and I talk about older women ... part of the conversation always is, 'Gosh, those women have had to give up so much to make those things happen. Should we give up those things?'" That's a good question. Perhaps it's answered by what Stewart sees in these older women. "I see so many women in their 40's and 50's who are struggling with [the question:] did they make the right decisions about their career."[28]

Right decisions. Every woman wants to make them, whether they are about a boyfriend, balancing work and home, raising children, a husband and marriage, a career, when to work and when not to, whom to believe and whom not to, setting priorities, what and whom to live for, planning life, or connecting with God. These are the right choices women want to make. The question is, Where is the counsel and the guidelines that can help achieve this outcome? This is what this book, *The New Eve*, offers.

Bold Moves

In the pages that follow, I want to set forth *five bold moves* I believe can help steer you or any woman of faith toward a more secure, satisfying, and God-honoring life. But let me also say that while these bold moves apply to women of any age or circumstance, I believe younger women in particular have the opportunity to benefit most. That's because these bold moves are much like financial investing. The sooner you get started, the greater the return.

I rejoice today that women like yourself have an unlimited canvas on which to paint their lives. Having two adult daughters of my own, Elizabeth and Rebekah, I love the new freedoms and opportunities our modern age offers. For instance, Elizabeth worked for a major consulting firm in Germany, traveled the world, and proved herself in leadership spheres formerly reserved for men. Rebekah got a master's degree, taught public school for several years, and is now an international teacher in Rwanda. But for my daughters, for you, and for women everywhere, I also desire one additional gift: the power to choose wisely. That's because wisdom has always been the balancing weight to freedom and opportunity. Wisdom is the school the first Eve failed in, but it's the one the New Eve seeks to excel in.

2

The View Behind the Choices You Make

What drives the choices you make? Have you ever thought about that? Most of us believe we script our lives, using a highly objective reasoning process involving facts, circumstances, and personal preferences. And while to some extent that may be true, there is also another, less conscious force behind your choices.

It is your *worldview*.

A worldview is the packaged past. It is the mind-set—right or wrong—you have assembled as your way of seeing and interpreting life. Call it your take on life—your selective spin rooted in deeply held convictions and beliefs, however they came about. It colors everything about you, including the way you experience life and perceive the reality around you. This is the power of a worldview.

Your worldview also shapes what you want life to be. It plots your future. It influences your plans and shapes your goals. The mind-set you have right now—your worldview as a woman—is a significant force behind the kind of woman you are and are choosing to become. Typically, one of four female-specific worldviews lies behind your choices that define your womanhood.

The Traditional Worldview

This is a worldview of nostalgia. It springs from a comfort with the lifestyle you grew up with and a desire to have that same lifestyle for yourself. New ideas, breakthrough opportunities, and changing social alignments are often viewed as threats to this more traditional way of life, so you quickly dismiss them, regardless of their merit. In this mind-set the past is always best.

Some women back into this worldview simply because the rapid pace of change in our world overwhelms them. Trying to chart a path in a world of confusing, ever-changing options becomes too much to handle, so they decide to stick to the well-worn ways of their upbringing. Mustering the will and wisdom to analyze alternatives and consider a better path may seem too risky or not worth the effort. And so they go with what they know.

Is that you? Is that good? Maybe, maybe not. But certainly it's easier that way. More familiar and predictable. Did Mom choose to stay at home and make that her sole aspiration? You can choose to stick with her tradition and do the same. Did Mom depend on your dad for everything? You can repeat that. Or did she rule your home and your dad? You can seek to repeat that too. Or, as is more likely in the younger generation, did Mom pitch herself into a career, devoting all her best energies to pursuits outside the home? If so, why think differently? Like mother, like daughter. It's only natural for you to be caught up in this same trajectory. Besides, most of your friends are probably running along the same line. And so you replicate. You carry on the lifestyle you grew up in, not because it's necessarily right or best for you but because it's what you're comfortable with.

The Wounded, Reactionary Worldview

Believe it or not, reacting to a wound can become your worldview. It can mark your life so powerfully that everything about you is shaped or interpreted by its persuasion. Such a wound can come from your parents' failed marriage, your father's abuse, your mother's neglect, your parents' misplaced priorities, or a personal tragedy. As a result, this wound now serves as the primary lens through which you see your world. Unlike the traditional worldview, which esteems the past, this mind-set demands that you become different from your past, sometimes radically opposite in order to protect yourself from previous experiences.

Many women embrace this worldview. Study the background of some of the most strident modern-day feminists and you will find women choosing a lifestyle tailored to distance themselves from the pain they experienced from men, most often from the man they love most—Dad. To establish security, these women grab for power and promote a radical ideology that shields them from ever becoming vulnerable to or dependent on men again.

Andrea Dworkin is a prime example. At nine years of age, Dworkin was molested in a movie theater by an unknown male assailant. When she married, her husband assaulted her with kicks, punches, and burns. He even bashed her head against the floor so hard she was knocked unconscious. It's no surprise Dworkin became a fire-breathing feminist who saw men as worthless and urged women not to marry. "Like prostitution," she wrote, "marriage is an institution that is extremely oppressive and dangerous for women."[1] Her tragic life became her worldview.

Elizabeth Cady Stanton is another example. The veritable founder of the American women's movement, Stanton was raised in an early nineteenth-century home that prized boys and looked on girls with cool indifference. The earliest memory seared into Elizabeth's mind was that of her parents expressing displeasure at the birth of her younger sister: "What a pity she's a girl!"

When Elizabeth was eleven years old, tragedy struck the family. Her elder brother, a promising college graduate and the lone jewel in the family crown, died in an accident. Seeking to ease her father's despondency, Elizabeth vowed to emulate her lost brother, especially to achieve his glories in academia. Greek would become her second language and history her passion. Since her brother's skills in the saddle once pleased her father, she would master the horse as well. Whatever her brother was, Elizabeth was driven to become to win her father's affections.

If these were her hopes, they were cruelly crushed. Mr. Cady was unable to see past his own grief and prejudice. "Oh, you should have been a boy!" was all the paternal tenderness he could muster.[2]

Elizabeth's sense of shame and humiliation at being a girl eventually created in her a powerful counteraction. Much of her subsequent life was spent attacking this warped valuation of her parents, which she saw everywhere. Everything, including the church and the Christian faith, felt her passion and biting wrath. "The whole history of mankind," she said, "is a history of calculated, organized tyranny over women."[3] That's a wound speaking, not reality. But as her worldview, it powerfully shaped her life.

Today many women choose a life for themselves from woundedness. So as not to be taken advantage of, or abandoned the way Mom was, they insulate themselves from vulnerability through the power of a career. Self-sufficiency becomes their driving worldview. So as not to be dominated by a man the way

Dad did Mom, they angrily reject their church and the Bible's teaching on male headship and become hard and demanding. Or to feel safe, they find a man they can dominate. To escape the pain of their parents' marriage, some women choose to use men and shun marriage. Or they reject men altogether and seek intimacy in the company of other women. Some women try to resolve the love deficit they suffered with their fathers by giving themselves to any man who shows interest. Others become superachievers in an attempt to overcome the stigmas of poverty, racism, and other social limitations they experienced in childhood. On and on I could go, but the point is this: a woman's response to past hurts can become her primary worldview, driving many of her life choices.

The "Whatever's-In" Worldview

The Bible speaks about this mind-set more than any other. Actually, it warns women about adopting this take on life. Paul said, "Do not be conformed to this world" (Rom. 12:2a). That's because despite the world's momentary popularity and the power of acceptance that goes with it (which we crave), being trendy in your lifestyle and mind-set rarely has long-standing value. Its power is in the moment. Unfortunately, whatever it offers you as *in* for today is usually *out* by tomorrow. And as its shine fades, it leaves you to deal with the consequences, either nagging emptiness or the serious pain of regret. And yet this is the worldview of choice for most people. Rather than think deeply or long-term about life, it feels right to go with the flow of culture and fit in, regardless of future costs.

Few women represent this worldview better than Jane Fonda. If you are in your twenties, you may identify Fonda only with movies. But her "life du jour" spans decades. In the late '60s during the Vietnam War, Jane teamed up with her draft-card-burning boyfriend, Tom Hayden (whom she later married), and joined the increasingly popular antiwar movement sweeping across America at the time. She soon made a name for herself as "Hanoi Jane." Magazine covers, newspaper headlines, TV reports—Fonda was at the forefront and in the spotlight.

Then times changed, and the war ended. So in the '70s Fonda found a new identity. She shifted her focus and added her voice to the growing women's movement. She threw away her bra and her short-term husband and became an empowered feminist.

Then came the '80s when fitness and the hard body took center stage. Jane once again changed with the times. She shed her business suit for a leotard. She pumped her fists for exercise rather than protest and starred in *Jane Fonda's Workout*, the top-grossing video of all time.

But times changed again. You can't be a hard body forever. Besides, in the roaring '90s rich was the new in. And one of the richest men on the planet was Ted Turner with his CNN empire. So Jane followed the moment yet again and set off in a new direction. "Once again I seemed to have become someone new because of a man," she would later say of her relationship with Turner.[4]

By decade's end Turner was gone, along with the greed that had swept through the '90s. With the stock-market crash, religion was now on the rise, especially the evangelical kind. And so as if on cue, Jane morphed with the times. In the late '90s it was reported she had found Jesus. Christians rejoiced. Unfortunately Turner made it clear he would have no part of a born-again Jane, so a divorce quickly ensued.

But Jane's evolution continued. By early 2005 she had come full circle and was protesting war again, this time America's involvement in Iraq. So where will she be next year? Who knows? But you can probably bet her life will center on whatever's popular at the moment.

Now I know Jane is an extreme example of this worldview. But I've seen worldliness do strange things to many people—Christian women included. This mind-set unleashes a deadly malignancy that undermines and compromises the purpose-driven life Christian women like yourself are meant to live. Without regular intake of God's Word to counteract this, your life will more than likely default back to worldly conformity. The magnetism of living for whatever's in is that seductive.

The New Eve Worldview

I chose this title rather than "Biblical Worldview" for a reason. Certainly not to discount the Bible. The New Eve worldview *is biblical*, but it is also *specific to women*. Women who embrace this worldview actively shape their lives around the Bible's gender-specific applications. In doing so, they become women who are more than "Christian" in name only. They go beyond being mere churchgoers who claim faith but whose choices, values, and lifestyles more closely reflect the nonbiblical worldviews previously discussed.

A New Eve takes God's Word seriously not just at church but in the everyday walk of life. She lets the Bible answer the big questions every woman needs to face. Questions like: What does it mean to be a woman? What should be my priorities as a woman? How do I balance my life? How do I avoid regrets? How do I please God? New Eves don't merely ask such questions. They find specific and practical answers and use them to color their choices, determine their life direction, and measure their progress. These answers become a fixed mind-set that builds for them a unique, fulfilling femininity void of many of the excesses and regrets that mark other worldviews.

Of course, you may be asking, Can a significant and satisfying twenty-first-century womanhood really be defined from

Scripture? One that can apply to *all* women and yet not be guilty of cookie-cutter sameness that presses everyone into a common mold? One that will stay fresh even as you grow older? One that can guide you to the best in life? The answer is yes.

In the chapters that follow, you'll find five bold moves drawn from the Bible that help you, as a woman, define for yourself the best life possible. They are:

- **Live from the inside out.**
- **Adopt a biblical definition of womanhood.**
- **Embrace a big-picture perspective on life.**
- **Live with the end in mind.**
- **Use wisdom with a man.**

These moves are not hard to understand, but they require boldness and courageous faith to activate. More importantly, they unleash the best of this life. They have worked this way in many women's lives, and they will work in yours as well. We'll unpack the first of these bold moves in chapter 4. But first let's look at the major issues women are struggling with today—issues these bold moves are meant to resolve.

3

What the Issues Are

To be good at counseling, you must have the ability to distinguish between issues and problems. That's a gift of insight most people don't possess. To them, issues and problems look and feel the same. They are not. In fact, they are as different as cause and effect. Problems are nothing more than "surface eruptions"— usually generated by a deeper, less apparent, unresolved issue.

For instance, you may have trouble relating to a certain individual in your family or social group. You fight. You don't get along. You can't communicate. Those are very real and serious problems. But the real *issue* behind that struggle may actually be a secret jealousy they hold against you or the need you have (but won't admit) to control other people. Issues, you see, lie behind problems. I've seen people contend all their lives with one difficulty after another but never identify or address the issue actually fueling their problems.

It's easy to have this blind spot. I know because I've fallen prey to it firsthand. I once brought in a highly regarded consultant to help me with a number of serious problems I was having in leading our church. For several hours I poured out to him my frustrations with staff, organization, time demands, directional challenges, and personal concerns. Honestly, I was really hurting. From time to time, he would ask probing questions to aid his understanding of my situation.

Eventually, I finished venting my list of nagging problems. I was eager to hear what ideas he would offer to help untie me from these leadership knots. Pen in hand, I prepared to take notes.

After a long pause he looked at me and said, "Robert, you're tired." I quickly acknowledged that but waited for him to get down to real answers for solving my predicament.

But that *was* his answer.

With laserlike insight, he rightly named the issue behind all my troubles. And as the day went on, he helped me see that most of my current undoing was either exaggerated or self-inflicted because of exhaustion. The reason I was so overwhelmed and confused was simply because I was out of gas. "Fatigue makes cowards of us all," he said. "What you need is some time off to recharge your batteries and put life back into perspective."

At that moment time off was the last thing I thought I needed. But his advice proved to be on target. And by heeding his wise counsel and addressing this issue—not working harder or smarter on the problems resulting from it—I found the real leadership help I needed to get my life back together.

When I talk to women about their personal problems, I often get an earful. And that's a good thing. Unlike men, women on the whole are much more transparent and open about the things that trouble and concern them. Along with speaking to women personally, I've also had the opportunity to formally survey hundreds of women across our country. These surveys have helped me better identify and understand the specific problems women say they are facing.

On the next page I've provided for you a detailed list of the struggles these women have told me. Let me suggest that you pause at this point and take your time looking this list over. Grab a pen or pencil and circle the hot phrases you can personally identify with. After you've completed this, we'll continue.

Problems Women Say They Struggle With
— Circle those that apply to you. —

- time management
- accomplishing goals
- making financial decisions
- taking care of everyone (even adult kids)
- figuring out what I should do
- parenting my children God's way
- security
- trying to fill all roles well
- balancing attention between children and husband
- redefining my life after divorce
- being allowed to be the biblical woman I want to be
- not enough time and energy to do all I want to do
- not knowing where I fit in
- being everything to everyone
- parenting teenagers
- direction and purpose
- feeling worthwhile as a homemaker
- organizing/prioritizing
- meeting my own expectations
- expectations of others
- not being so assertive
- maintaining focus
- time vs. money
- not doing enough

- what to do with the rest of my life
- living with a difficult, angry man
- being average
- balancing motherhood, career, and marriage
- being left alone
- missing out on my kids growing up
- failure as a mother and woman of God
- not having left a legacy for someone
- loneliness, isolation
- growing old
- not reaching my potential
- not having skills to support myself if I suddenly had to (and not wanting to)
- financial security, retirement
- a bad relationship with a man
- making sure I'm all that I can be
- wondering where my marriage is going
- being a good mother and wife
- intimacy
- really trusting God
- finding a godly man who is not intimidated by me
- being 36 and single
- relationships
- feeling inadequate

- making it
- failure
- raising my sons without a father presence or role model
- working full-time
- proving myself
- learning who God wants me to become
- handling power struggles at work
- my job
- saying no
- contentment in finances
- marriage that gets harder as years go by (25 years)
- single mom trying to be everything
- guilt
- abusive marriage
- thinking outside myself and my needs
- questioning if I'm a godly wife and mother
- my identity, discovering who I am
- what to give my life to
- choosing the best
- staying faithful
- not understanding men
- thrown into working world after divorce
- finding boundaries of independence/freedom
- trusting my husband's choices
- really loving my husband

- no help with children or elderly parent
- not making a difference
- wasting my talents, gifts, time, and energy
- my children saying I didn't do a good job
- finding my new focus as empty nester
- missing significant moments with my children
- not fulfilling my purpose as a woman
- not doing "it all" right
- raising children
- my purpose as a single woman
- not feeling appreciated
- having to work without job experience
- intimidating others by my strengths
- vulnerability
- directionally placing my life steps
- always comparing myself to others

- being in the world but not of it
- defining my role as soon to be married
- communication
- not being consumed by the drive other single women have for corporate advancement
- not finding the right husband
- feeling social pressure to be career-oriented vs. family-oriented
- moving past failure
- gentleness in a strength-driven workplace
- independence vs. submission
- staying focused on God in an ungodly world
- overwhelmed with responsibility and lack of time
- insecurity or dealing with other worries
- being myself
- indecision
- overcommitment

- having children
- living my life selfishly
- making good choices
- that I'll regret my choices when I'm old
- finding respect, significance, and value as a stay-at-home mom
- foolishly wasting time, money, and energy in the wrong direction
- that my daughters won't know who they want to be as women
- having no discernible identity outside my family
- being content with God's plan if it differs from my desire
- discerning where to devote my time
- insignificance
- wrong priorities
- other:
- _____
- _____
- _____

The words you've just circled are your problems. But if I can play counselor for a moment, let me suggest that most of these problems, even as painful as some of them are, are not the *source* of your troubles. Most of what you and other women struggle with today actually springs from *five volatile issues* that often remain open and unresolved. And by remaining unresolved, they infect life with confusion and bad decision making. On the other hand, when these issues are addressed with biblical convictions (which we will do beginning in chap. 4), many of the problems flowing from them naturally work themselves out or can be successfully dealt with.

So what are the issues behind many of the problems swirling around and within the lives of women today? Let's take a look.

Issue 1: An Ever-Evolving Femininity

What does it mean to be a woman today? You would think such a basic question would be easy to answer. Think again. No commonly accepted answer exists. Certainly not one with biblical roots. Even the images *woman* brings to mind have morphed significantly over the last generation. Fifty years ago when you heard this word, you were more than likely to associate it with words like *soft, sensitive, submissive, nurturing, pretty,* and *virtuous.* Not so today. Words like *assertive, strong, confident, sexy, independent,* and *equal* have inserted themselves into the modern picture.

Added to this are new assertions of what it means *to be* a woman. Hillary Clinton set the tone for the new woman when she quipped on her husband's 1992 campaign trail that she was not about "to stay home and bake cookies" and "be some little woman standing by her man." Actress Sharon Stone went ever further. She reportedly said, "As I see it, the choice today is between being feminine and equal. I choose equal." Everywhere today new voices like this are redefining and reshaping what it means to be a woman.

As a Christian woman, you cannot help but be influenced by the sweeping sociological changes presently taking place. Indeed, in our postmodern world it's easy to think of being a woman as nothing more than a personal choice. But *if* you are a woman of faith, personal choice should first yield to deeper questions, such as: How does God define me as a woman? Is there a basic pattern for womanhood that supersedes my preferences and choices with divine call? I believe the Scriptures offer life-defining answers to such questions for any woman who has the ears to hear. But that's for later.

Here the issue is the significant status changes that have marked the lives of women since the 1950s. They have been as dramatic as the changes in women's hairstyles. While salons during this time moved from the beehive to Charlie's Angels to "the Rachel" and beyond, a woman's social identity has shifted as well from one role paradigm to another, as illustrated below.

The Swinging Social Pendulum

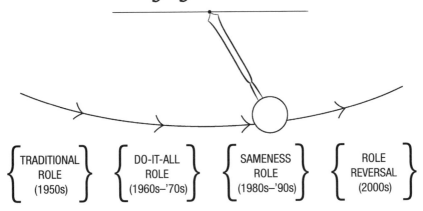

$$\left\{ \begin{matrix} \text{TRADITIONAL} \\ \text{ROLE} \\ \text{(1950s)} \end{matrix} \right\} \quad \left\{ \begin{matrix} \text{DO-IT-ALL} \\ \text{ROLE} \\ \text{(1960s–'70s)} \end{matrix} \right\} \quad \left\{ \begin{matrix} \text{SAMENESS} \\ \text{ROLE} \\ \text{(1980s–'90s)} \end{matrix} \right\} \quad \left\{ \begin{matrix} \text{ROLE} \\ \text{REVERSAL} \\ \text{(2000s)} \end{matrix} \right\}$$

The Traditional Role

Typified by the sitcoms of the 1950s, this was an era of Ozzie and Harriet, strict social decorum, well-defined and separated gender patterns, and patriarchal authority. Young girls played with dolls, put on practice teas, and paid close attention to etiquette. In school they studied hard enough, but very often their primary aim was to wed and have a family. The sooner, the better. Women who desired to pursue careers outside the home were rare. So were single women. "A woman's place is in the home" was the slogan that carried the day. That not only meant that a woman best served society by getting married and staying home with her children, but it also strongly implied that a woman should leave the broader world of professional ambitions to men. This stereotype was spiritually endorsed by many churches as being *the* biblical model of what a woman should be, despite biblical examples to the contrary (Judg. 4:4; Prov. 31:16; Acts 16:14; 18:1–3, 26).

My mom went a different direction. She married late and continued to work full-time as the office manager of a law firm even after having three boys. And though she had to hire help to care for us when we were young, the close proximity of her office and the gentle pace of a small southern town allowed my mom to miss little, if any, of my adolescence. I never thought my mom wasn't there for me. She was. But she was also the exception as a working mother in the '50s. Most women were stay-at-home moms.

The Do-It-All Role

Social mores were shattered in the radical '60s and the psychedelic '70s. In this era almost everything for a woman came into question: her role, her place, her value, her virginity, and even the sacred ground of marriage. Why not merely live together? It was a wild time of free love for many women and men, and some unfortunately paid for it later. But at this moment freedom from traditional restraints was intoxicating.

Married women were liberated too. They were told they could have it all, especially when it came to work and home. "If I have to, I can do anything. I am strong, I am invincible, I am woman," proclaimed Helen Reddy in her hit song. From this age of idealism, the concept of the supermom was born. This idea, however, was short-lived. By the end of the '70s, working moms were tasting the bitterness of reality and exhaustion that doing it all brings.

One such mom confessed to Oprah Winfrey, "I tried hard to be the supermom, but frankly I wasn't good at it. Looking back, it was costly. I had a very angry little girl who wanted her mommy, and I didn't have the time, and I didn't know how to balance it. It took me a long time to understand that you can't have it all."[1] And so as quickly as it had arisen, the supermom concept crumbled into the supermyth. But there was no going back to the '50s. A new womanhood had been uncorked, and if supermom wasn't the answer, then something else was.

The Sameness Role

In the '80s and '90s a new form of femininity arose. One more realistic but also more aggressive and assertive. Women would no longer try to do it all. Instead, they would demand that men share every facet of life with them fifty-fifty. Away with gender distinctions at home, work, and play! Columbia University's Carolyn Heilbrun argued for this idea in her book *Reinventing Womanhood.* A husband's career should not take priority over his wife's, and his care-giving duties at home should match hers exactly, said Heilbrun. She justified her "symmetrical family" model on the claim that gender differences are a sociological contrivance, not the result of divine design. A mom's tender femininity reflects the manipulative forces of social persuasion, not her nature. And if men balk at being motherly, it's the culture, not nature, that's to blame. The no-roles sameness model was "scientific," said the social critics, and "destined to be the dominant family form of the future."[2]

Adding fuel to this flame for Christian women was the emergence of Christian egalitarianism. This new theological movement within the church espoused "sameness" among men and women as God's ideal before sin entered the world. This theology soon caught fire. Men were no longer to be the heads of their homes or the overseeing leaders (that is, elders) of the church. Role differences were out—even sinful. Everything was to be shared equally—fifty-fifty.

While all this sounds fair and balanced, the problem is men and women are *not* the same. Equal in value? Yes. Equal in sharing God's divine image? Absolutely. But we are different by God's design (Gen. 1:27). And those differences mean something, both practically and theologically, whether or not we want to face it.

During this time women also encountered another hard lesson. As they sought to be like men in the workplace and vied for promotion and advancement, they learned something men had long known: companies want *more*. The concept of sameness may have advanced many women's professional lives, but after hours it quickly became a home breaker. And children were the ones wounded by it the most. In truth some career women have ended up becoming the very person the 1950s homemaker chronically complained about in her husband: he works too hard, he's gone too much, he's home too little.

So how can a working woman make home and career work for her? For many women that's the million-dollar question. For other women the social pendulum has moved on to something new—role reversal.

Role Reversal

As the twenty-first century breaks upon us, a new evolution of woman is arising. It's a feminine transformation defined by a social realignment occurring more frequently between men and women. And what exactly is that? Simply this: men and women are switching roles. It's the '50s traditional model in reverse. More and more women are leading the men in their lives. More and more women are the primary breadwinners of their families. And more men are working less and staying at home with the kids. Newsmagazines confirm that this is a growing trend.[3] Thirty-four percent of men polled say they would consider staying at home if their wife earned more money. Studies show that of the fifty most powerful women in business, a third of them have "trophy husbands," men who stay at home full-time to take care of domestic duties. More broadly speaking, 51 percent of the men whose wives outearn them do the majority of the domestic work. *Businessweek* magazine assessed this trend by concluding, "Finally, more career women are getting the one thing they say they need most from their husbands: a wife."[4]

For men this spells an identity crisis of the first order. A *Newsweek* article bears this out, for with few exceptions the stay-at-home dads who were interviewed confessed their dislike of this new role. Why? Because from earliest boyhood, males fix their eyes on the broader world outside the home, where they have a God-made hunger for adventure and accomplishment. Women too are exhilarated by success, but for men it is the very stuff of life. Men who aren't conquering the turf God has called them to aren't merely standing still; they're losing ground and their masculine soul in the process. Something dies inside a man when he gives up on authentic manhood and settles for something less than the call that lies within him. His manhood becomes hollow. And when a man surrenders his life and leadership to a woman, as Adam did to Eve (Gen. 3:6, 17), both inevitably hate it in the end.[5]

So where does this swinging social pendulum leave you as a woman? Honestly, with hard choices concerning . . .

- What you want out of life
- Balancing home and career
- Living with a man
- Children and what is required for them to grow up healthy
- Your spiritual beliefs

But underneath all these concerns that you and other women battle with daily is a basic question rarely asked or answered: How do you define what a woman is and isn't? For you as a Christian woman, we could add: How does God define what a woman is and isn't? When those questions are left open and unresolved, confusion, wrong turns, and painful regrets usually follow. But an amazing clarity, confidence, and problem-solving ability comes when you can move past confusion to solid, life-giving answers. Defining your womanhood at a basic level is *the issue* behind the challenges and problems of an ever-evolving femininity. It's an issue we will address from a biblical perspective in chapter 6.

Issue 2: A New Supreme Pursuit

Let's face it: life today, especially for young women, has been turned upside down. A radical and profound idea has been introduced and propagated concerning what womanhood is really all about. Against all social history as well as the wisdom of Scripture, young women are bombarded with slogans and images in the media, taught from grade school through the university, and told indirectly by what they see honored among women that *a career is the ultimate goal in life.*

This is womanhood's new supreme pursuit against which all else should be measured. We celebrate "Take Your Daughter to Work Day"; we guard girls against stereotypes that make motherhood and domestic life seem like their inevitable calling; and every time we speak to them about aiming high, we're thinking of careers in medicine, law, business, or the like, possibly inviting them to put off or deny altogether some of their most powerful, God-given drives. Former Brandeis professor Linda Hirshman pressed for this new pursuit when she wrote, "Housekeeping and child rearing [are] not worthy of the full-time talents of intelligent and educated human beings."[6] Her book for today's woman is appropriately titled *Get to Work*.

I recently attended a high-school football game in a rural Arkansas town. It was the essence of small-town Americana. Picket fences, a general store, folks gathered on the front porch to solve the world's dilemmas. The game was homecoming, and at halftime the announcer introduced the members of the homecoming court. For each of the young ladies he mentioned their accomplishments and future aspirations. Doctors, lawyers, bankers, teachers . . . the aspirations were high and career oriented. Nothing wrong with that. A career is a good thing. We can all be proud when our daughters aim high in accordance with their gifts. But as I sat in the stands, I began to wonder how the crowd might react if one of the girls had named motherhood or homemaking as her chief ambition. Honestly, it would have sounded odd. Second-rate.

In the twenty-first century the primacy and place women individually and collectively give a career is a huge issue with immense consequences. And what women decide—what *you* decide—depends on how some deeply philosophical questions are answered: What should be the supreme pursuit of my life? Around what should everything else in my life be ordered? We will address those questions in chapter 4.

Issue 3: Successfully Engaging a Man

If engaging a man feels as if it has become more difficult, it has! Stephanie Coontz, the author of a comprehensive book on the history of marriage, says, "Relations between men and women have changed more in the past thirty years than they did in the previous three thousand."[7] Traditional relational pathways have become tangled and confused. Polls indicate the greatest pessimism women have today is about their love lives. Single women around me keep asking, "Where have all the men gone?" They are frustrated and bewildered at the timidity and passivity of modern men. A recurring complaint is that men no longer take the initiative. They seem to run from it as if from an infectious disease.

On many college campuses "the date" is becoming extinct. *New York Times* columnist David Brooks shares the following personal encounter he recently had with a group of students. "One night over dinner at a northern college, a student from the South mentioned that at her local state university, where some of her friends go, they still have date nights on Friday. The men ask the women out, and they go as couples. The other students at the dinner table were amazed. The only time many young people have ever gone out on a formal date was their high school senior prom. You might as well have told them that in some parts of the country there are knights on horseback jousting with lances."[8] More and more with men, young women are having to step forward first to make the call, take the lead, and be the pacesetter in the relationship.

Women are also changing the ways they engage men. Casual sex is up; so is living together. So is having a family *without a man*. Today a record 37 percent of all new moms are unwed, many by choice. The most dramatic increase is with women in their twenties. "More American women than ever are putting motherhood before matrimony," reported *Newsweek* writers Debra Rosenberg and Pat Wingert.[9]

Unmarried women are today's fastest-growing demographic.[10] And when you do meet a man you desire to commit to, what are the rules of engagement that will make the relationship last? Do you know? Does he agree? What are the roles, yes *roles*, you will play in your new life together? If you think they will be the same, think again. The so-called fifty-fifty arrangement is always in the eye of the beholder. What you say is my fifty, I may feel is my eighty and vice versa. Who keeps score?

So what are the conditions that bring a man and a woman together in happiness? A host of problems arise when you don't know. That's why we are going to tackle this important issue in chapters 10 and 11.

Issue 4: The Challenge of Motherhood

What does it take to be a good mother, especially when a career is mixed in? The "mommy wars" pitting working women against homemakers has marked the deep divide that exists over this issue. It's one loaded with hard choices, intense feelings of guilt (real or imagined), personal ambitions, and economic necessities. We will address this issue at length in chapters 4, 7, and 8.

Being a mother is like being a nurse, chef, guidance counselor, mediator, teacher, playmate, policeman, and air traffic controller all rolled into one. If stay-at-home moms struggle to fit all this into a single day, mothers who work full-time outside the home face even greater challenges. The hardest-working people anywhere are career women who double as moms. A *USA Today* poll revealed that 60 percent of working mothers would choose to stay at home if their financial situation permitted it.[11] But financial concerns often rule this out. Today 60 percent of women with children under the age of six are working outside the home, the very time when social scientists and child psychologists tell us that children need maximum attention and nurturing from their moms to ensure sound intellectual, social, and emotional development. There is simply no substitute for healthy, engaging "face time" with a child. And children need lots of it from their parents to feel good about themselves and about life. This reality will not go away, no matter how much a woman earns or provides for them.

Today's working woman feels this dilemma and the guilt it often brings. The pressure and the toll of trying to juggle children and career ambitions have become so great that a new trend is developing in America today: young women are choosing to have fewer children or none at all! A record number of women ages fifteen to forty-four report that they actually intend to forgo motherhood. Most often it's a lifestyle decision. A growing number of couples now rate the value of their work, recreation, and standard of living above that of having children. Anne Hare is one example. According to an AP reporter who interviewed her, "Hare and her husband made a momentous decision three years ago: They would not have children. It's not that they don't like kids, she says. They simply don't want to alter the lifestyle they enjoy."[12]

The 2000 Census Bureau report indicates that the birthrate in America is the lowest in our history. It currently stands at 2.06 per couple. At this rate American parents are barely managing to replace themselves. Immigration is the only reason for America's robust growth. For increasing numbers of women, opting for motherhood is no longer automatic or even a top priority.

For a Christian woman God's command to "be fruitful and multiply, and fill the earth, and subdue it" in Genesis 1:28 has not gone away. Rightly understood, it is a sacred charge to commit oneself to raise and launch a healthy next generation that is able to bless the world (our communities and our cities) with the righteousness of God. For Christian women the question should not be, Will I choose to embrace this God-given command? but rather, Do I know (or want to face) what my children really need from me to grow up healthy? In our demanding, fast-paced, pricey, career-oriented culture, wisdom and the courage to make hard choices are now absolute necessities for addressing this crucial issue of motherhood. Without them you can expect your kids to have the same kinds of problems you see through-out society today.

Issue 5: The Maze of Unlimited Choices

I remember the lively interaction I had with a futurist back in the late 1980s. As a researcher, his job was to assess specific kinds of data that could reveal coming cultural changes. In our discussion I asked him pointedly what he considered to be the most significant change looming before us. I don't know what I expected, but his answer surprised me. "Choices," he said. "The greatest change and challenge in the next generation will be in dealing with the plethora of choices you will have."

His prophecy is now your reality. Today as a woman, you have unlimited choices as well as the freedom to pursue them. As we discussed in chapter 1, this is both a blessing and a curse. It's a blessing because now more than ever, women can pursue their dreams. But it can also be a curse because the reality of so many choices demands a new skill many women (and men) lack: the ability to choose rightly.

One of America's greatest thinkers, the late Peter Drucker, made the following observation shortly before his death in 2006. He wrote, "In a few hundred years, when the history of our time will be written from a long-term perspective, it is likely that the most important event historians will see is not technology, not the Internet, not e-commerce. It is an unprecedented change in the human condition. For the first time—literally—substantial and rapidly growing numbers of people have choices. For the first time, they will have to manage themselves. And society is totally unprepared for it."[13]

Let me personalize Drucker's insight for you with the follow-ing points:

- • Large numbers of women (you) now have choices.
- • As a woman, you will have to learn to manage yourself.
- • Most women (maybe you) are totally unprepared for how to do this.

Your life as a twenty-first-century woman is no longer fixed and one-dimensional, where you grow up, get married, have children, end of story. No, today your life is wide open, fluid, multidimensional, and besieged by choices and options. Pamela Norris underscored this reality when she wrote, "Women are still trying out different plots at different stages of their lives. There is no definitive path to tread, just multiple possibilities."[14] All of this shouts a huge question: How do you manage these options, choose between them, and not get burned by big regrets?

Everyone needs help when it comes to navigating this maze of unlimited choices. In chapter 9 we will offer practical ways for you to get your hands around it.

Conclusion

Most of the problems women deal with today spring from the five issues I have introduced in this chapter. My experience has been that many women never come to terms with them. Instead, they expend their energies battling circumstances flowing from these issues, many times with very few positive, long-term results. A better way—one that unleashes a better life—is the one that can identify these issues and find sound solutions for each of them.

This is the path a New Eve chooses to take. She is a woman who knows the issues and has discovered how to address each in practical, real-world ways that work for her. As a result, she is a woman who is able to define her womanhood with biblical conviction, is clear about what she is living for and why, has wisdom and know-how in engaging a man and raising children, and possesses a biblical grid for making good choices and finding a healthy balance. In short, a New Eve is a woman who has learned how to manage her life. And she has done so by employing five bold moves, the first of which we will now explore.

4

A Gender Journey into Genesis

Years ago America was captivated by the television mini-series *Roots*. Based on the best-selling book by Alex Haley, the series followed one man's riveting quest for personal identity. As a black American, Haley longed to know his family history. Where had he come from? What were his people like in their original setting before slavery and subjugation cut them off from their culture and took them away? To find answers, Haley traced his ancestral heritage to its beginnings in early Africa. The whole premise of his journey was this: unless you understand where you've come from, you can't fully appreciate or accurately grasp who you are now. The past is crucial to the present.

In this sense Genesis is to the human race what *Roots* became to Alex Haley—a helpful piece of personal history we must understand if we want to rightly orient our lives to the present. Here preserved in print are the social and spiritual roots common to every race of humans. The first three chapters of Genesis in particular offer us helpful insights. They summarize in story what the rest of Scripture labors to explain and resolve. With each verse we discover truth about first moments, first purposes, and first life. Here at the headwaters of both history and the Bible, we grapple with the fundamental explanations behind why we are the way we are. We can believe it or disbelieve it. But here we are offered a user-friendly way of understanding what life is really all about, including God's purposes for gender. It's all here in the Genesis "myth."

The Genesis "Myth"

I know what you're thinking. *If Genesis is a myth, why look there to find answers for my life as a woman?* Good question. Let me begin answering it by noting that *myth* is not synonymous with *fiction*, as we often assume. Webster's dictionary defines a myth as "any real or fictitious story that appeals to the consciousness of people by embodying ideals or realities." Did you hear that? Some myths are *real!* Genesis is that kind of myth—a real story about real people and real events.

But real or not, all myths are special. That's because they are used to establish standards for life against which we can define and measure ourselves. For instance, what woman comes to mind as being America's gold standard for feminine sexuality? What woman's sensuality is part of our cultural lore? Her posters are still found hanging in shops and restaurants, and her story is still being told in books and on TV. She courted presidents and sports stars and still fires the fantasies of men everywhere as the icon of erotica. You know who she is, don't you?

Or what woman do you think of as the embodiment of selfless service to others? Who is legendary for giving her life away as a doer of good works?

Even though Marilyn Monroe and Mother Teresa are no longer living, we nevertheless point back to them in their respective areas as standard bearers against whom we can define and measure ourselves now. This is what *real* myths do, and this is exactly the sort of myth Genesis is. Its historic events, now preserved in story, offer us an even bigger reality. As our roots, Genesis defines life as God meant for it to be. Every word and phrase in this summary account of creation is loaded with meaning. In fact, the most vital realities of your life as a woman today can be measured against the coordinates set down in the Genesis myth.

What Genesis Says about Gender

Perhaps the most important thing Genesis teaches us is that God created everything. Life is no cosmic accident, and of all the things God created, none is more meaningful than *you*. You stand as an equal with man at the apex of God's created order. In Genesis 1:27 we read, "God created man in His own image, in the image of God He created him; male and female He created them." Here we learn that women and men were designed to reflect God's image over the rest of creation. But just as important is what lies at the heart of this design. Of all things it is gender: female and male.

The thing you as a modern woman must first decide is whether you believe this central tenet of the Genesis myth. This is a crucial first divide for living life. Did God create you special, and is your gender purposeful, or are you merely a product of random chance? Your decision here has huge ramifications for how you proceed in life and view your femininity. Of course, you can choose to believe that everything exists by pure accident and that nothing has a fixed purpose. If that's you, then you are left to create your own definition of womanhood. On the other hand, if God created the universe as Genesis says He did and you believe it, then you find yourself called to embrace a breathtaking dignity and fixed meaning to life and to your womanhood. You are purposeful, designed, intentional, and

God has put you here because He is out to achieve something in the gender He has wrapped you in.

Core Callings

In Genesis you find what I call universal "core callings" for every woman. By core callings I mean gender-specific purposes God has in His mind for you as a woman—purposes around which everything else you do and choose in life finds its rightful place and order of priority. In Genesis these core callings are *the same* for every woman. Men are no different. They too have core callings that are the same for every man.

The reality of universal core callings does not mean God intends for all women to be identical. Quite the contrary. One woman will always differ from another because of other factors that make up her life. The way you look, your personality, your special combination of gifts, abilities, and capacities, your wants, desires, and choices all ensure that you will be someone entirely unique. But Genesis is not about what is unique to you as a woman but rather what is common and enduring for *all* women. It embodies God's timeless standards against which every woman can measure her life and, when necessary, readjust to.

Genesis presents three core callings for women to build their lives around. One or more of them will always apply to you, regardless of which season of life you are in. These are the feminine directives God designed for you to embrace as the bull's-eye of your life. Genesis 1:28 says, "God blessed [Adam and Eve]; and God said to them, 'Be fruitful and multiply, and fill the earth, and subdue it; and rule over the fish of the sea and over the birds of the sky and over every living thing that moves on the earth.'" In this mythic verse God set forth two of His three core callings for you as a woman.

Be Fruitful and Multiply

This core calling refers to reproduction, and though there are cases (some very painful) in which women cannot or will not bear children, most will become mothers. And here God is saying more than "Make babies." Rather, as with the animals, He intended for Adam and Eve to replicate "their kind" (Gen. 1:24–25), which means humans who are in harmony with Him, as Adam and Eve were in their original state, and who extend His righteousness throughout the earth. God in effect is saying, "Produce God-glorifiers." He charges the first couple (and us) to expand the power and beauty of His image by multiplying it in others throughout the earth. That this is a part of what it means to "be fruitful" is seen when the rest of Genesis and all of Scripture are taken into account (for example, Deut. 6:7; Ps. 78:5–7; Eph. 6:4). God wants men and women to become moms and dads (barren couples can accomplish this through adoption) who rear and nurture healthy, well-adjusted, life-giving image bearers as the next generation. That's a breathtaking core assignment for you as a woman, and it will demand nothing less than your spiritual authenticity plus well-honed parenting skills and a selfless attitude.

Subdue and Rule

God is also a concerned environmentalist. He wants all aspects of life on this planet—social, spiritual, and physical—to be improved by the hands of His people. Theologian John Stott said it this way: "God makes us, in the most literal sense, 'caretakers' of His property."[1] By using the word *subdue*, Genesis says the earth actually needs the rule of godly women and men if it is to be set right and made healthy, balanced, and orderly.

This truth of Genesis was illustrated to my wife and me a few years ago when we bought a home whose landscaping had been sadly neglected. The front and back yards were literal jungles. The earth had been left to its own devices. What it produced was overgrown, unkempt, and unattractive. After my wife and I set our hands to it for several hard months, a transformation occurred. Flowers grew in place of weeds. Order transplanted chaos. We had subdued our small part of the earth, and the earth was better for it.

I believe our concern for order and beauty is God-given, rooted in the original call to subdue and rule. We have all been entrusted by our Creator to be difference makers on this planet (Ps. 115:16). And that difference making extends far beyond a well-kept lawn and garden. At a much higher level we are also called according to our gifts and talents to the more challenging tasks of helping people, improving society, enacting justice, sharing the gospel, and advancing God's kingdom in our communities. Jesus even taught us to pray this way: "Your kingdom come, Your will be done, *on earth*" (Matt. 6:10, emphasis added). As a woman, you have the primary core calling to allow your femininity to grace the world with these things. God has designed you for specific good works (Eph. 2:10). Just as the earth needs the cultivating hand of humanity to draw out its greater beauty, so too society needs the gifts of the feminine heart—your heart—to make it better in a myriad of ways.

Rita O'Kelly has discovered one of those ways. Rita is not only an executive with a major investment company but also a Kingdom builder. Despite a demanding schedule, she makes time to mentor a number of younger women in her firm before work and during the noon hour with her wisdom and godliness. She has helped a number of these women achieve more than bigger paychecks; she has helped them make wise decisions for their careers and families, overcome personal roadblocks, and find better balance and direction for their lives.

Connie Phillips, a homemaker, became involved in a local public school several years ago. Seeing needs beyond those of her own kids', she helped establish a mentoring program that today reaches into thirty-one area schools with one thousand volunteers and touches more than six thousand students.

These are only two examples of what I believe God had in mind for women when He said to subdue and rule. Women hold a unique power to make life better, and in the beginning God named this as a core calling for all women—including you.

Leave and Cleave

A third core calling is companionship—a deep, lasting intimacy with someone of the opposite sex. With rare exceptions God has designed you for a man, whether he's arrived in your life yet or not. You see this goal in Genesis 2:24, when God said, "For this cause a man shall leave his father and his mother, and shall be joined to his wife; and they shall become one flesh." Here God created a superbond called marriage. No other human relationship can compare to it in either intimacy or durability. As I said, most women have been created for this experience. According to statistics, more than 95 percent of you will find a mate.[2] If you're not married yet, this should give you great hope during your present waiting period.

It is true, however, that some will never marry. Others will marry but then find themselves alone again because of death or divorce, in some cases never to marry again. How does the calling to leave and cleave apply to them? In a word, it doesn't. Either because of a particular life circumstance that has no remedy or by some special calling of God, this Genesis directive is set aside. In such cases your responsibility is to narrow your focus to the remaining core callings God has for you—to the goals of multiplying God's glory in your children (if you have them) and/or in making a Kingdom impact with your gifts in the lives of people you touch in the part of society in which God has placed you. These core callings do not change, regardless of your marital state. In addition, the apostle Paul pointed out in 1 Corinthians 7 that a life of singleness or a season of singleness can actually be a special time of Kingdom opportunity for women. He wrote that the woman who is no longer married, as well as the virgin who has never married, can leverage her singleness to give "undistracted devotion to the Lord" (vv. 34–35).

In Genesis, God set forth three specific directives that, with rare exceptions, apply to every woman's life. We could paraphrase these three feminine core callings as follows:

Leave and Cleave
You are to seek deep, lasting companionship with a man.

Be Fruitful and Multiply
You are to raise up and launch healthy, godly children into the world.

Subdue and Rule
You are to advance God's kingdom on earth in ways specific to your gifting.

This is what God had in mind when He made you and all other women in His image. These core callings are to be at the center of your life. Any woman who embraces these core callings and pursues them as top priorities orders and manages her life in a way that is meaningful, satisfying, and, most important, eternally connected. Here a woman submits to her Creator's wishes for her life. And from here, from these roots, He richly blesses her.

Core Callings in Perspective

It's important to note that these core callings represent only a *part* of your life—a crucial part, to be sure, but only a part. Please hear that. Much more than these callings makes you who you are. The relationship between your core callings and the other elements forming your unique identity can be diagrammed as follows:

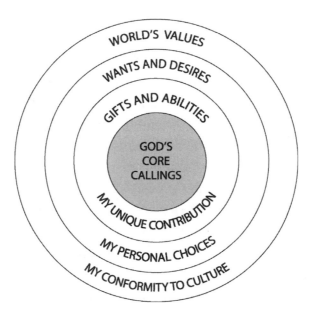

Notice as you move outward from the core, you come first to *gifts and abilities*. This is where your life expands beyond the sameness that Genesis says covers all women. Here you encounter those first aspects of identity that make you unique. You may be an artist, an athlete, musical, extroverted, a high-capacity achiever, a leader, administrative, numbers oriented, people oriented, an encourager who relates to people deeply, a helper, or an entrepreneur.

On and on we could go, but the point is this: you are by God's design your own snowflake, etched in a pattern never to be repeated in the whole history of women.

Next comes the level where your *wants and desires* are found. Your autonomy as an individual and your personal choices come into play here and further separate you from that core sameness you share with other women. Here you decide what other things will define and shape your life as a woman, that is, what experiences you want to have, what people you want to be with, what things you want to do, and what dreams you want to pursue.

At this level, it's important to remember that the choices you make around your wants and desires have consequences—good and bad—when it comes to fulfilling God's core callings on your life. For instance, your choices and the pursuits that spring from them may complement these callings; they may create conflict or impose roadblocks in fulfilling them; or they may foster circumstances that keep one or more of these callings from ever happening. Whatever direction your life ultimately takes, much of its unique script is written here by the decisions you make.

The third level is where the *world's values* reside and where cultural forces seek to shape, manipulate, and form your life into certain prescribed patterns. This ring often unleashes godless values wrapped in stylish images, and it does so by relentlessly bombarding you through music, media, academia, and popular opinion to gain your allegiance.

Here you are told what you should look like; what standards you should embrace; how you need to arrange your personal, career, and domestic priorities; and what you should believe about womanhood. Here the world constantly presses to choose for you how you should think and live. Without a conscious effort to combat this pressure, it's amazingly easy to give in to it.

Your Lifestyle Direction

Although the diagram on page 49 can summarize your life, something else is needed to show how you actually live as a woman. Generally speaking, the life-shaping power of a woman's life flows in one of two directions—either from the outside in or from the inside out.

Let's first address outside-in living. Many women live primarily by the dictates of the world's power and influence. Maybe you live this way more than you know or would like to admit. As I said, it's a current that's hard to resist without conscious effort.

Outside-In Living

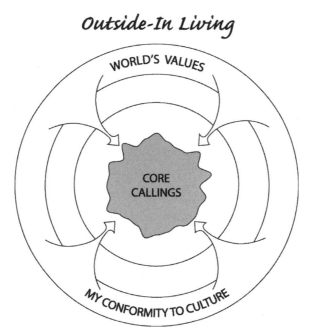

When you live from the outside in, the world's values and the cultural conformities that go with them will dominate almost everything about you. This outer ring will squeeze and reshape all the inner rings of your life into its mold. Your wants and desires, personal choices, what you do with your gifts and abilities, and your beliefs about your core callings all shift onto the tracks set down by the world's priorities. From here you yield to cultural images and measure your life by the themes of your favorite movies; the ideas in the latest best-selling books; the images in magazines; or the opinions of your favorite educator, politician, or social trendsetter. You are driven by your senses—what you see, hear, and feel—not by well-defined spiritual convictions. When you live this way, your core soon bears the twisted influence of the outside world. And when the outside world changes its values, or presents new options and opportunities, you shift again, always working to make your inside fit the outside.

But this doesn't work. Instead, you experience problems and conflict. You may even experience lifelong regret. That's because by living from the outside in, God's core callings for your womanhood have been compromised, dumbed down, or choked out altogether by a new set of worldly outside callings (see Mark 4:18–19). Some Christian women live this way more than they know and wonder why life is so troubled and conflicted.

Outside-in living was never God's design. Romans 12:2 says it straight up: "Do not be conformed to this world." *Do not!* For you as a Christian woman today, that's a tall order with so much being offered to you by our modern world. Besides, since the day Adam and Eve rebelled against God, humans have gravitated to this kind of living. It has become our nature to believe the world's ways are better than God's ways. Outside-in living is naturally our first choice.

But outside-in living exacts a heavy toll on women. It reshapes and molds life to fit values and attitudes that are not native to the true femininity God has placed within every woman's heart. To go against this divine grain is an invitation to heartache. Our roots in Genesis shout this warning. Women who forsake their core and choose the forbidden fruit of this world find that in time it leaves them lonely or angry or childless or with angry children or with an angry husband or with no husband or empty or with everything but true happiness. Outside-in living looks delicious on the front end, but it has a deadly back side. Just ask Eve.

There is a better way, and a number of women are living it. It's found in heeding a courageous call to live from the inside out. Nothing is more spiritually fundamental to a woman's life or as powerful.

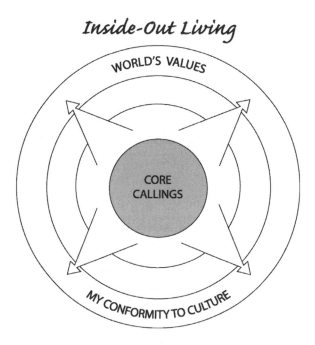

Inside-Out Living

This is not a call to withdraw from the world. It is an appeal to you as a woman to let God's core callings be your starting point in every area and in every decision of your life. Remember, these callings are divine *commands*, not suggestions. They are meant to shape your world, not be shaped by the world. They are, from a biblical perspective, the sacred nonnegotiables of your life.

They are meant to be your guardrails for living in the modern world. As such, they are constantly in your mind to measure and direct the choices and pursuits of your life and in which direction you need to readjust if necessary. While you will certainly enjoy a wide variety of activities, interests, and opportunities that engage your gifts, abilities, wants, and desires, here's the point: never, *ever* make choices at the expense of being true to your core callings.

Over the years I have had the pleasure of observing many women who have embraced by faith these core callings of Genesis. They have made them their dominant reality and let them successfully guide the seasons of their lives. For example:

- The emergency-room physician who leveraged her considerable professional skills not for more money but for less work. A new mom, she negotiated a three-day work week that provided her a way to invest deeply in her daughter and her patients.
- The homemaker who as an empty nester retooled and surprised everyone by becoming an award-winning real estate developer. With a new, more public face, she is now making a Kingdom impact on her community both with her savvy business skills and with her witness for Christ.
- The businesswoman who altered her career to better balance her relationship with her husband. Her willingness to help him has made both of their lives better.
- The scores of working moms I know who, with their husbands' support, made the difficult choice of stepping away from their jobs to stay home with their children. For many, life from a material standpoint became leaner and more financially challenging. At times the budget shortfalls were downright painful, but these difficulties were

outweighed by the joy of being a greater part of their children's lives.

All of these women chose to live from the inside out. Each, in her own way, is a New Eve.

Then there's the journey of my friend Rebecca Price. As an outgoing, lively new Christian in college, Rebecca expected she would someday have a husband and children. But instead of sitting on the sidelines until that happened, Rebecca rightly decided to follow her gifting and passions and do something to serve God's kingdom. So after college she began a career in Christian publishing. Gifted with a good sense of what it takes for a book to succeed, Rebecca quickly proved her value. Her career expanded, and with it came greater opportunity. "But all during that time I always thought that one day I would get married and have kids," she said. "Career was never my driving force."

But as time passed, the opportunity for marriage never materialized. Eventually Rebecca was faced with this question: Do I live freely as a single, or do I live waiting for a man? The answer from the Bible seemed clear: trust God and live freely as you are. Courageously, Rebecca embraced that answer and soon found herself being used in new and exciting ways. Doors for furthering the reach of Christianity through publishing opened on the West Coast, in the United Kingdom, and in Africa. Companies such as NavPress, Word, and Multnomah Publishing called on her expertise. And when Random House, the world's largest English-language trade-book publisher, wanted to develop a Christian imprint called WaterBrook Press, it looked to Rebecca to serve as the vice president of marketing.

Now fifty-five, Rebecca has begun daring new Kingdom adventures with her friend Lisa Bergren, such as their first book, *What Women Want: The Life You Crave and How God Satisfies*.[3]

As for marriage and children, those are things God has not brought into her life.

"I think one of the first questions I'll have for God in eternity is, Why did You not choose for me to have kids? I have to admit that I really don't understand why it has turned out that way for me."

But this doesn't mean Rebecca is living with bitterness or regret. Instead, she has focused her life and her gifts even more intensely on God's core calling of Kingdom building. "It was important to me to be content with what my sovereign God has called me to, and that is what I've done. And I feel blessed to see how God has used me and my singleness to further His purposes." One thing Rebecca wants single Christian women of every age to hear is this: "Don't take the short view. Women tend to do that and feel despair over not being where they want to be. Be active instead of passively waiting for life to change. By 'active' I mean pursue God, pursue love, and pursue excellence. Figure out how God can use you *now*."

I appreciate Rebecca's courage and bold faith. This is inside-out living at its best. When you keep God's core callings in focus, ordering your outside according to your inside, life will increasingly gain momentum and freedom. It invites God's blessing. On the other hand, embrace the outside-in way of life, and you are most often ordering up a serving of dead ends and regrets. I hear this from women all the time: "Why did I think life was all about me? Why didn't I take God's Word more seriously? Why did I wait so long to try and have children? Why did I relate to men the way I did? Why did I think my husband could make it without my help and involvement? Why didn't I invest my single years in something more productive? Why did I believe my kids wouldn't notice I wasn't there?"

It doesn't have to be this way. But it will take bold moves on your part to secure a better outcome. As I told you earlier, these bold moves are in essence big-picture faith strategies to help you successfully navigate the challenging terrain of the modern world. Rather than just guessing your way through life as so many women do, these bold moves help point the way to a wiser and more satisfying life. So now that our gender journey through Genesis is complete, here is your first bold move for managing life successfully as a New Eve:

Live from the inside out.

The first Eve, of course, went a different direction. Her story in Genesis 3 stands as history's most convincing witness to the wisdom of inside-out living . . . but for all the wrong reasons. So let's take a look.

5

Eve and the Fall

Past to present, the landscape of womanhood has included many history turners. These are women of uncommon influence who have changed the world by their unique imprint and left it a different place.

Esther was one such woman. When she was called from obscurity by a Persian king who needed a wife, her shrewdness and courage as his queen saved her fellow Jews from execution and extinction. Another history turner was Florence Nightingale. In an era when medicine was considered "man's work," Florence went against the grain and pursued a career in health care. Through hands-on involvement in wretched medical clinics and military infirmaries, she discovered that poor sanitary conditions were the root cause of many needless deaths. Today, nurses and doctors all over the world trace their life-saving emphasis on sanitation to Ms. Nightingale. Then there was Rosa Parks, a courageous black woman who took a front seat on an Alabama bus and changed race relations in America forever. There were many others: Susan B. Anthony, Margaret Mead, Emily Dickinson, Joan of Arc, Queen Elizabeth I, Harriet Beecher Stowe, Catherine the Great, Indira Gandhi, Cleopatra . . . the list goes on and on.

History is full of women who have reshaped our world in one way or another. But no woman has turned history so significantly or as permanently as the first woman: Eve.

Eve's first claim to fame is simply that she was the mother of us all. Interestingly, biologists now believe this. Recent discoveries in genetics have led scientists to conclude that all humans are descendants of the same woman. The proof, they say, is in our shared mitochondrial DNA. In a *Time* magazine article titled "Everyone's Genealogical Mother," Michael Lemonick writes, "If family trees were charted indefinitely backward, they would eventually converge on a small group of ancients who were ancestors of us all. Now biologists suggest in a report to *Nature* that a single female living between 140,000 and 280,000 years ago in Africa was the ancestor of everyone on the earth today. Inevitably—and to the probable delight of creationists—many scientists are calling her 'Eve.'"[1]

Yes, Eve was a real person. Hard science is edging closer to the biblical plotline. And while DNA now offers us a genetic link to her, Genesis 3 offers us a much fuller picture. So take a look. No, you won't find her physically described there. You'll have to imagine that for yourself. In your mind's eye you may see her as I do: as a dark-haired beauty with strong physical features; sharp wit; and an energetic, determined personality. But the social and spiritual images of Eve in Genesis 3 are eye-popping. These pictures have been purposefully preserved for you and for women of every generation to gain insight. Look closely enough at them, and you'll even notice traces of yourself in Eve. Yes, you are a unique individual, but at the same time, it's important to recognize your connectedness to your supragreat-grandmother and how she predisposes you as a woman to certain tendencies, traits, and temptations. That's why Eve is so important. Her past is your present.

Options

In Genesis 3 Eve discovered for the first time that there was something else in life besides God's will and calling for her. Life had options! Everything was not fixed or guaranteed. Choices could be made.

Offering one major option was a crafty serpent with an exceptional marketing strategy. In their encounter he pressed Eve from the outside to abandon those callings God had given her to embrace on the inside. And the emotional buttons this serpent pushed to tempt her in that direction should sound familiar to every modern woman.

- God and the man speaking for Him are holding you back. Don't you know that?
- You've been lied to.
- Do you call this fair—having these limitations placed on you?
- Can't you see how second-rate you are right now? Why are you doing this to yourself?
- It's time for you to take control of your own destiny and maximize your potential.
- You need to know that what you don't have is so much better than what you do have.
- Stop worrying; you won't die if you strike out on your own. You'll excel!
- Don't let others keep you from your best.
- You can have it all!

Theologians will tell you this serpent was actually only a puppet. Speaking through it was the master of all evil we know today as Satan. In the wonder of the original garden, a snake was certainly an appropriate disguise for Satan to use to approach and engage the first woman. In this agrarian setting it made sense. But to target modern women, the puppets for marketing Satan's voice have had to change. Talk-show hosts, movie stars, college professors, advertising agencies, songwriters, authors, and social critics do nicely. These outlets are craftily manipulated and appropriately placed for maximum impact. But the messages themselves have not changed. Look at them again. Today's tempting voices use the same old Genesis 3 pickup lines. And every modern woman who listens to them becomes Eve all over again.

Satan's deception of Eve brought us to a cataclysmic moment that today still affects us all. Most of us know it simply as the Fall. It was a moment when all of God's original intentions and core callings for you as a woman (and for me as a man) became twisted, distorted, and—most of all—difficult.

What the Fall Unleashed

Genesis 3 should have featured Adam in the starring role of a courageous protector. After all, he was supposed to head this relationship with the same loving leadership with which Jesus would later cover His church (Eph. 5:23). Instead, Adam was strangely missing from this dramatic scene as Eve dangerously entertained the serpent's overtures. Where was he? The tragedy is, he was actually around, though we will have to look closely in this moment to find him. After six long verses of satanic dialogue with Eve, we finally catch a brief glimpse of Adam. Almost as an afterthought, Genesis 3:6 says he was "with her." In other words, the whole time this evil madness was being unleashed on Eve, Adam was right there, watching his wife's strength wane as Satan deceived her into abandoning God's command not to eat the forbidden fruit.

We are not told why Adam was so passive in this life-or-death moment or what he was thinking, but we can guess. Clearly, Adam was no dummy. He was an ingenious, creative, natural-born leader designed by God to rule the world. He was also keenly aware of what was happening and what was at stake. For those reasons it seems clear that Adam was testing God and selfishly using his wife to do so. By letting his wife take the fruit without his direct involvement, Adam had already reasoned that he would win, regardless of the outcome. If she ate and died as God had previously warned (Gen. 2:17), he could profess innocence by not having participated. On the other hand, if Eve ate and didn't die, then Adam had proof that God was, in fact, holding back on what was best for them. In that case Adam still had time to join his wife in this new life. Obviously, Adam thought he had outwitted everyone, including God.

It was a huge mistake.

The truth is, as Adam stood and watched his wife entertain sin, *he* sinned! Not overtly but covertly. Adam denied God even before Eve's deception was complete. He shunned his leadership responsibilities, he abandoned his helper, and he embraced evil in his heart. But rather than outwitting God, he discovered a higher reality he should have known: "God sees not as man sees, for man looks at the outward appearance, but the LORD looks at the heart" (1 Sam. 16:7).

This doesn't mean Eve was innocent in these events or a victim of them. She knew the rules, but she freely and fully disregarded them. As the conversation advanced with the serpent, it was clear to her that Satan was calling her to make a momentous decision that went contrary to her design and God's clear commands, and yet she continued to take ownership of the situation. She disregarded her husband too. Rather than looking to Adam and insisting that he take his rightful place as her head, she made this fateful choice alone. Then, after she ate, she turned to her husband and instructed him to do the same. Sensing that Eve had gotten away with it, Adam complied.

In a tragic role reversal, Eve led, Adam followed, and the world fell. Spiritual death, not a better life, immediately descended on Eden, and humanity's relationship with God was severed.

Along with this separation from God, gender wounds were also unleashed on Adam and Eve and on their posterity. Authentic manhood became mangled. The negligent and selfish passivity Adam displayed in the Garden now becomes the passivity of all men. Everywhere you look today, you see men take charge in sports, business, and politics. They are aggressive warriors when it comes to their personal pursuits.

But when it comes to social and spiritual responsibilities, passively standing there like the original Adam becomes more their norm. The wife waits for her man to lead at home, but after a while she falls into prodding him: "Let's go to church. Let's do something with the kids. What about our relationship? Where are we going in life?" His response is the same as Adam's was to Eve: "You decide. You lead. You take the responsibility. I'll watch." It never fails that when I say things like these to a male audience, the men hang their heads because they know it's true. In the substantive things of life, social and spiritual, men are naturally passive. It's our inheritance from Adam.

Authentic womanhood also took a major hit in the Garden. Eve lost her feminine nobility when she fell into Satan's deception. And precisely as Adam's passivity still lives in men today, Eve's vulnerability to deception still carries on in all her daughters. In every generation women are enticed with the same forbidden fruit: to neglect, compromise, or abandon altogether

God's core callings for what the world convincingly promises is better. If anything, the deceptive fruits of a modern world are more plentiful than ever before, and as a woman, you are naturally prone through Eve to take and eat. This is the inheritance Genesis says Eve leaves you—the tendency to believe that there is something better out there for you to pursue than what God has already prescribed. But it's all a painful lie.

The fall also created a new reality of woundedness between men and women. Life between the sexes is cursed and infected with personal agendas and power plays. Look at God's words to Eve in Genesis 3:16: "In pain you will bring forth children; yet your *desire* will be for your husband, and he will *rule* over you" (emphasis added).

You will miss the significance of this divine pronouncement if you don't stay with this verse word by word. Pay special attention to the two words I highlighted in italics. The "desire" God said Eve will now feel for her husband and the "rule" Adam will now exercise over her are both desperate and tragic. They are corruptions of God's original design of Adam as a caring head and Eve as a supportive helper. Because the first couple chose to abandon God's design for them, every future man-woman relationship will be undermined with difficulty. That includes yours and mine. These corruptions are at ground zero of the struggle we often refer to as the battle of the sexes.

For us to fully grasp what the "desire" of woman is, we need to look at Genesis 4:7, where this puzzling word is used again in a more revealing context. How it's used here helps us unlock its meaning in Genesis 3:16. Notice in chapter 4 that God was speaking to Cain, Adam and Eve's firstborn son, after the young man had developed a murderous attitude toward his younger brother, Abel. At this point God said in verse 7, "If you do well, will not your countenance be lifted up? And if you do not do well, sin is crouching at the door; and its *desire* is for you, but you must master it" (emphasis added).

Did you catch that? Here "desire" is clearly associated with the idea of *control*. God told Cain that sin sought to control him. That was its aim. And this understanding of desire helps us unlock Genesis 3:16. The desire to control in Genesis 4:7 is also the woman's desire in Genesis 3:16. This means that even with the true love a woman will have for her man, the consequences of the fall will taint this love with an unholy struggle. From this point on, a woman's calling as helper will be mixed with the desires of a competitor.

In response to this controlling desire that every generation of women must now deal with, Genesis 3:16 says a man will seek to rule. This is not a reassertion of the noble leadership God set forth for Adam in Genesis 2. This is a cursed leadership—the kind that dominates, forces compliance, and demands submission. The Hebrew word used here often described the rule of kings. It is a rule of power, not love. It is an injurious rule men have used over women for centuries.

Here's the point: because a man and woman are cursed, true intimacy between them is no longer a given. Love is now mixed with an inevitable power struggle, which, if not properly addressed, can reduce their initial passion for each other into an onerous contest of wills. Eve was cursed with the need to control: "your desire will be for your husband." Adam, on the other hand, meets her evil desires with his own corruption: "he shall rule over you." What was once a harmonious dance between the sexes now becomes a subtle (or not-so-subtle) fight for supremacy.

Unfortunately, that fight not only undermines the core calling for deep companionship God intended for couples, but it also severely impacts parenting and the core calling of raising and launching a godly, healthy next generation. As in so many families today, the dysfunction Adam and Eve unleashed on themselves through their choices eventually expressed itself even more adversely in their children. In Genesis 4 we watch as their two boys grew up confused, angry, and contentious. The crescendo came when a jealous Cain slew his brother, Abel. The life God originally intended to unleash through the fruitfulness of this first couple ended tragically in violence and death, as we see in many children today.

Eve, who was promised so much more by the serpent, was now left with a life of deep regret. Choosing to live from the outside in, she became *the* symbol of a failed and futile femininity for all women of every generation.

Nevertheless, she continues to have her followers. There are many thousands of them in every age. Countless other "Eves" who, like her, still choose to believe God's core callings can be short-changed or neglected in the pursuit of other, seemingly life-giving ambitions. And in those pursuits *helper* is cast aside as an antiquated concept whose time has past. Children are worked in around a career by women who still believe they can do it all. The pursuit of worldliness washes away authentic godliness and even common sense. As for the first Eve, the outside dictates everything and brings the same failures and heartaches.

So what's a woman to do? If you are wise, you will learn from Eve and not repeat her mistakes. You will enjoy many of the opportunities our modern world offers but never at the expense of God's core callings on your life. No, when it comes to those, you choose to live courageously from the inside out. That's because New Eves are known for bold moves, not foolish ones.

A Bold New Eve

Of the women I know, few have had to make a bolder move than Terry Jones. When Terry was in college, she had no idea of the adventure and opportunity that lay just around the corner. The spark that ignited it was when Terry and three of her friends decided to start a Christian singing group in 1990.

It was all fairly simple and fun at first. A few singing opportunities in area churches gave the girls experience, exposure, and the thrill of seeing God work through them. But in a very short time the impact of their ministry in music took off and began to attract national attention.

In the explosion that followed, their singing group, known as Point of Grace, sold more than five million albums; produced twenty-four consecutive number-one singles, two platinum records, and five gold records; and won eight Dove and two Grammy awards. They were voted the 1994 New Christian Artist of the Year and the Christian Group of the Year in 1996. As their popularity grew, Point of Grace would perform as many as twenty concerts a month. Terry was on top of the world!

In 1994 Terry married her college sweetheart, Chris. That is when a tug-of-war broke out in Terry's heart. As much as she loved the ministry of Point of Grace and the Kingdom influence it was offering her, she loved Chris more. But the professional demands of touring and recording made "loving Chris more" hard to live out.

The arrival of children further complicated matters. First there was Cole, then Luke, and finally Mallory. Like most modern women, Terry worked hard to balance her home with her career. But she confessed, "To wear the mom hat, wife hat, famous-singer hat, businesswoman hat, recording-artist hat, and be-nice-to-fans hat started taking its toll on Chris, me, and the kids. I would literally spend most of my time packing and unpacking, washing, cramming seven days of housework into two or three, and then packing up myself and the kids to leave again." On one tour Terry and the kids packed sixteen suitcases to take with them.

"It was a very hectic schedule; many of my days were planned to the minute," Terry said. "The hour on stage was wonderful, but it was only one of the twenty-three it took to get there."

The small nudge Terry first felt trying to manage her life as a wife, mother, and professional now grew into a raging storm. Even with courageous adjustments of paring back on concerts and touring schedules, Terry still found herself running in circles. "It just wasn't working," she admitted. She and Chris weren't together enough. There was never enough time to focus on the kids.

And then there was the Holy Spirit. For years Terry had been increasingly aware that His voice had been asking her to focus in this season of life on her core callings as wife and mother. But to leave Point of Grace was not merely leaving a job. In Terry's words, "It was leaving an identity, a way of life. No more concerts, no more three-hour conference calls, no more flights to Nashville. Is this what God wanted?"

Terry prayed and sought counsel, but most of all, she struggled. Not with what God was telling her to do—that was now clear. No, Terry struggled with what would happen if she obeyed: suddenly being left out, falling behind, the loss of an identity and recognition, setting aside her considerable talents, and of not being able to have it all.

It was an "Eve moment."

Terry would later say, "This was the hardest thing I had ever done in my life—to stand and go against the grain. I learned that when you do something God desires for you, it can be gut-wrenching, but a true, underlying peace drives you on." Jesus would call it "the narrow way." I call it living from the inside out, managing opportunity with wisdom. And so with white-knuckled faith, Terry elected to be a New Eve rather than replay for the billionth time the life of the old one. She retired from Point of Grace in March 2004.

So what drives her now? "Freedom," she says. That internal conflict that dogged her for so many years is gone. In its place is the freedom to live life without guilt or regret. Her new life, of course, is not without its ups and downs. At times her "ordinary life" wishes for the glamour of her former one. But Terry is a woman at peace with God because she has chosen in this crucial season of life to give her best to His priorities. She is at one with what eternity says matters.

In a final good-bye in Point of Grace's e-newsletter, *Heart to Heart*, Terry wrote the following: "To my family . . . now I can wake up every single morning and go to bed every night knowing every part of your life. I LOVE being your mommy and Chris, I LOVE being your wife."

Terry Jones . . . living from the inside out.

6

The Power of Gender Vision

Vision energizes life. It inspires. It clarifies. It harnesses the powers and abilities of one's life and focuses them on a prescribed end. That's because vision is a forward thing. It's out there calling you ahead to new growth and fresh opportunity. A life that is called forward by a positive vision is a life of health and passionate movement. Conversely, a life that is not called forward will stagnate or fall backward into trouble. Life becomes aimless, twisted, and disoriented. Without vision people naturally tend to wander. Bad decisions follow. We all know such stories. It's the friend we visit in rehab, the coworker whose life is in constant crisis, or the sister who doesn't come around anymore.

One of Scripture's most powerful maxims says, "Where there is no vision, the people are unrestrained" (Prov. 29:18). The word *unrestrained* is worth noting. In the one other time this word is used in the Old Testament, it describes what Moses observed when he returned from Mount Sinai with the Ten Commandments. While he was away on the mountain, the people of Israel had turned to idol worship and pagan revelry.

Exodus 32:25 then says, "Moses saw that the people were *out of control.*" This is exactly what happens when people lose sight of where they should be going in life. Where there is no vision, life gets out of control.

The same is true when it comes to gender. Without a gender vision men and women have trouble separating life-giving pursuits from mistakes and mirages. There is nothing specific, male or female, to aspire to, strive for, or check ourselves against. "Am I a good woman?" "Did I behave like a man today?" We ask such questions all the way to our dying day. Unfortunately, where there is no vision, there are no clear answers to such questions. And today we are paying a heavy price for this gender darkness, as are our sons and daughters.

A Gender Vision of Manhood

Several years ago I asked a group of men to help me formulate a succinct definition of biblical manhood. It sounded like a simple enough task. You would think we could have easily reached down and produced a statement of compelling clarity and unassailable truth, but in reality our efforts only highlighted our confusion. It was like nailing Jell-O to a wall. We simply couldn't do it.

So for months afterward I searched the Scriptures for an answer. How does the Bible define a man, a *real* man? What I eventually uncovered was a vision of manhood inspired by history's two most influential men. Both are called Adam, the Hebrew word for *man.* Both have left indelible marks on the human race. At times Scripture plays them up as opposites—two men who made radically different choices and pursued equally different lifestyles. But when they are brought together *as men*, they provide us with a way to envision and define biblical manhood.

The first of these two Adams is, of course, the Adam of Genesis. He was the original prototype male. He rolled off the factory floor divinely fitted for masculine success. Strong, intelligent, favored by God—the whole earth was his to rule as viceroy to the King. He was set for a great adventure. All he had to do was get three things right.

1. Adam had a *will* to obey.
2. Adam had *work* to do.
3. Adam had a *woman* to love and care for.

These were Adam's responsibilities as a man. But as we have already observed in our previous chapter, Adam failed on each of these counts in one fell swoop. Standing under the boughs of a forbidden tree, he refused to obey God's will; refused to do the work of manly leadership; and, in utter selfishness, despised his wife. His mistakes come down to one simple theme: he lost his masculine focus. And without this noble vision he became passive. Sadly, this visionless masculinity and the passivity that goes with it have become the plague of all men since.

Generations later, a second prototype male was rolled out. The New Testament refers to him as the second Adam, literally "the second man," but we know him by his more familiar name: Jesus. The Gospels make it clear that Jesus is God the Son, the Creator of the universe, and humanity's only hope for salvation. But they also make sure we know Jesus was *a man*: flesh and blood, mind and heart—exactly like every other man who ever lived. And as history's second Adam, Jesus unveiled a new vision of masculinity even as His life paralleled the life of the first Adam with the same three responsibilities.

1. Jesus had a *will* to obey.
2. Jesus had a *work* to do.
3. Jesus had a *woman* to love and care for.

Like Adam, Jesus the man was obligated to submit to the will and work of God. He also had a woman to love. Scripture calls her the bride of Christ. She is the church—you, I, and every Christian. The question to be answered now becomes, How will Jesus' new masculinity supersede Adam's failed one?

As with Adam, a garden was the scene of Jesus' greatest test. It was *the* moment for both His life and His masculinity. All his God-given responsibilities converged on a night of grief and betrayal. Set before Him was God's way and, of course, the other option... *my* way. Vision called Him to submit to His Father's will even though it would cost Him unspeakable agony and death. Adam's example, on the other hand, offered Him another option: release this vision and choose passivity over responsibility.

You know how the story ends. To paraphrase Romans 5:15, through one man (Adam) the world cascaded into death, but through a second man (Jesus), the way of salvation and new life was opened to all. So while Adam failed his manhood test in the Garden of Eden, Jesus triumphed with His in the Garden of Gethsemane. "Not as I will, but as You will," He cried (Matt. 26:39). Rejecting passivity, He selflessly loved his bride and bravely took a stand for His responsibilities even though it cost Him everything. He obeyed the Father's call because He trusted the Father's promise that the suffering of the cross was a necessary part of the journey to greater glory. "For the joy set before Him," Jesus endured the cross, Hebrews 12:2 says. In the end Jesus' courageous leadership showed all men what the first man's didn't: God's will, however difficult it may appear or feel at any given moment, ultimately results in a richer, more abundant life and greater reward. This was the vision Jesus held on to in modeling a thoroughly masculine life.

So it was in bringing Adam and Jesus together that I discovered a vision of manhood worthy of any man's consideration. By noting the parallels between these two towering masculine figures, their points of departure, as well as the different responses each had to his specific manhood responsibilities, I pieced together a biblical definition of manhood that now gives vision and inspiration to thousands of men who have tested it against Scripture. Here it is:

> *A real man rejects passivity, accepts responsibility, leads courageously, and expects God's greater reward.*[1]

A Gender Vision of Womanhood

Several years after developing this biblical definition of authentic manhood, I was asked by the women's ministry coordinator at our church to develop a series of messages on biblical womanhood. Right away I wondered, *Does Scripture provide for women a pattern for envisioning biblical womanhood like that of Adam and Jesus?* Put another way, *If Jesus is the second Adam, is there a second Eve?* Almost as soon as I asked that question, I had my answer.

Mary.

This special woman presents herself in such a way as to be considered Eve's righteous twin. Any serious reader of Scripture can't help but notice this. The Bible is arranged in such a way as to actually invite this conclusion. Much as Eve is on center stage in the high drama opening the Old Testament, Mary stands in the spotlight in the powerful events opening the New Testament. In different ways both are clearly the feminine counterparts to the two Adams. Both women help unleash history-making social and spiritual influences and leave as their legacies one-of-a-kind marks on the human race. Eve's foolish choices are used to introduce sin and death into the world. Conversely, Mary's courageous choices play a central role in helping to bring forgiveness and life back to the world. Eve is the model of an outside-in lifestyle; Mary, the model of an inside-out lifestyle. Eve and Mary—Mary and Eve. So striking are the obvious parallels between these two women that early Christians in the first three hundred years after Christ actually considered Mary to be a "second Eve."[2]

Unfortunately Mary rarely invites this healthy comparison today. Instead, for many Christians, she has become a controversial figure. Because she was the mother of God, opinions about her vary and often go to extremes. Some have held her in such high esteem as to actually worship her, while others react to this exaggerated adoration by retreating to the opposite error of ignoring her altogether. Some feel compelled to warn others that Mary is really nothing special. It's really a shame. As the famed New Testament scholar A. T. Robertson once said, Mary has long been "the victim of circumstances that have obscured her real character."[3]

But character is what makes Mary stand so tall in Scripture and among women. She exuded exemplary virtue and bold, extraordinary faith. Indeed, she lived the life the first Eve forsook. But even more important for our purposes, Mary's life, when coupled with that of Eve's, helps us to fashion a biblical definition of authentic womanhood.

Making the Comparison

When Mary's life is placed next to Eve's, I believe three significant issues stand out that serve as building blocks for constructing a vision of authentic womanhood.

What They Embraced

Both Mary and Eve were offered the chance to accept or reject God's word. In Eve's case God's commands could not have been clearer: be fruitful and multiply, subdue and rule, leave and cleave, and do not eat from the tree of the knowledge of good and evil, or you will die (Gen. 2:17, 24). With those core callings and a single restriction, Eve was free to enter all the goodness God had put before her and Adam. And Eden, the most idyllic paradise on earth, was just the beginning of that goodness. In truth, it was merely a launching pad for adventures yet to be revealed.

But this goodness soon was challenged. As we observed in the previous chapter, Eve heard from the serpent that there were better things beyond God's will for her—things she thought would be much more satisfying. God had been holding these things back and lying about them too. "You surely will not die!" the serpent scoffed while holding up the forbidden fruit (Gen. 3:4). Satan was telling Eve, the only thing that will die is your limitations. To eat is to become like God, to live life without restraint, to make your own rules, to decide for yourself what's right and what's wrong.

So Eve listened. And she responded by choosing to believe the deceiver's offer rather than embracing God's callings and the goodness she already enjoyed from Him. "There must be more," she concluded.

Mary's crossroads were even more daunting than Eve's. Seriously. Remember how it began? The angel Gabriel invaded Mary's home with his awesome presence (Luke 1:26–30). He seemed more threatening than inviting. The universal reaction to angelic visitation in the Bible is fear. Angels scared people stiff.

Take the priest Zacharias, for instance. He was in the temple of God when an angel visited him. Did he clasp the angel's hand and trade banter? No, Zacharias froze in his tracks (Luke 1:12). It is a fearful thing to stand in the presence of holiness.

And so here was Mary, a young girl alone at home, betrothed to a good man, minding her own business, and suddenly she was confronted with a supernatural encounter that might have ruined her life. God had made her pregnant before marriage! But He gave her His promise that this pregnancy of bearing the Son of God would make her life special too. It was an awkward, overwhelming moment. It sounded wonderful, but it also could have been a catastrophe. There was a real world out there that frowned on unmarried, pregnant teenage girls. After this encounter Mary could have easily panicked and submitted to an abortion (they were available in her day and popular among the Romans) or to a secret divorce (Joseph was willing to do so; Matt. 1:19), or she could have beat a trail out of town, leaving God's calling far behind. But Mary instead showed remarkable faith. She stood her ground, trembling and yet bold, and chose to embrace God's calling on her life. Mary's cousin, Elizabeth, summed up Mary's choice this way: "Blessed is she who believed that there would be a fulfillment of what had been spoken to her by the Lord" (Luke 1:45). As in Eve's case, this was Mary's life-defining moment. But whereas Eve shunned God's word, Mary embraced it.

What They Did

Action flows from belief. What you do reflects what you believe about yourself, the world, and God—your worldview as we discussed in chapter 2. We've seen what Mary and Eve chose to believe. Now what did they *do?*

In Eve's case it can be summarized in two words: she ate (Gen. 3:6). In this daring act she abandoned not only God but also the vital core callings He had set forth to bless her life: to be a helper to Adam, to nurture the next generation, and to be a Kingdom builder. All of that richness was abandoned for the promise of grander things as the fruit touched her lips.

Mary's choice of trusting God's word led to a completely different set of actions. She didn't strike out on her own or seek to end her pregnancy. In fact, she did just the opposite. She drew closer to God, cherished her pregnancy, and carried through with her marriage to Joseph. In spite of the fear she felt and the shame and misunderstanding that she knew would follow, she courageously aligned her life with God's callings. Nowhere is that alignment better seen than in Mary's remarkable statement, "Behold, the bondslave of the Lord; be it done to me according to your word" (Luke 1:38).

What They Expected

Both Mary and Eve expected good to come from their beliefs and actions. In making her break, Eve obviously envisioned even greater personal fulfillments and adventures than God's regime could provide. Her imagination, no doubt, ran wild. *What new freedoms will being like God give me? What wonders will knowing everything, good and evil, open to me? How much greater will I be? How much happier?* Here was the life she'd been missing, though before this moment she never once thought *anything* was missing. But now, caught up in the serpent's words, it all sounded too good to pass up. So she went for the life she believed could offer her more than God had given. And indeed she found more—more pain, sorrow, and regret than she knew existed.

Mary expected great reward too, but in her case it circled back to what God had promised her. We admire the courageous obedience she displayed, especially when we know the major payoff is still a number of hard years away. But Mary's faith held firm to God's word. Amazingly, she exulted in God's goodness to her before any of the really good results came to pass. In Luke 1:48–49 she said, "He has had regard for the humble state of His bondslave; for behold, from this time on all generations will count me blessed. For the Mighty One has done great things for me; and holy is His name." Mary was celebrating God's goodness at a time when all she could reasonably see was the scandal that would soon visit her. She was about to be a social outcast and a cause for gossip. Yet with the eyes of faith she trusted God and believed her life would be blessed with His best. Nine months later that's exactly what she got.

So here are the lives of history's two most important and influential women. Eve and Mary are *the* women of the Bible. In reviewing their divergent responses to God, to temptation, and to what each considered the better life, I find a biblical definition of authentic womanhood that I believe offers vision to any woman's life. Here it is:

A real woman embraces God's core callings, chooses wisely,
lives courageously, and expects God's greater reward.

What This Means to You

Let's unpack each phrase of this definition from a twenty-first-century perspective.

Embraces God's Core Callings

Those callings should be clear to you now. Namely, a woman is to pursue deep companionship with a man; launch healthy, godly children into the next generation; and advance God's kingdom in ways appropriate to her gifting. These are the callings around which the rest of your life should be prioritized, organized, and managed.

When any of these three goals are neglected or sacrificed by you as a woman for whatever reason (overemphasizing one goal at the expense of the others or compromising or abandoning one or more of these goals for other ambitions), trouble is usually waiting on the road ahead.

As mentioned in chapter 1, Sylvia Ann Hewlett set out to

write a book about a dozen women of what she called the "break-through generation." These are trailblazers who broke through bias and barriers to get their fair share of male-dominated fields. As these women were turning fifty at the dawn of the new millennium, Hewlett wanted to know their perspectives now that they were comfortably on top and had the chance to look back down their path to success. Several themes were common in all the interviews: an emphasis on education, unmatched ambition, and long hours. But after a while Hewlett noticed another theme shared by each of these women: all of them were childless. A dozen women, zero babies. Hewlett found she was on to something. She had selected these dozen women because each of them had reached the top. The odds that all of them would prove to be childless seemed impossibly long. But a little more research revealed that the odds are actually *high*. Today a whopping 49 percent of women business executives earning $100,000 or more annually are childless.[4]

As Hewlett turned greater attention to the childlessness of her interview group, the women became "guarded, even evasive," but they couldn't hide their feelings for long. One after another they admitted a deep sense of loss.[5]

What went wrong? Simply this: you cannot sacrifice any of the goals God has given you as a woman without loss. God created you this way. In her study of working women, Lisa Belkin noticed that a growing number of high-achieving women are leaving the workplace for motherhood. "There is nothing wrong with money or power," she said, "but they come at a high price. And lately when women talk about success, they use words like satisfaction, balance, and sanity."[6] A real woman will do her best to find a balance that allows her to be successful, not only in a career but also in all three of God's callings for her life.

Chooses Wisely

The modern world's dizzying array of opportunities and options constantly vie for our attention and affection. This makes choosing harder than ever before. Because we don't want to miss out on anything, it's natural to try and do everything. Unfortunately that grab-for-all-you-can lifestyle leaves most women in a state of near exhaustion. One woman confessed to me, "I am spread so thin right now, I don't think there's anything left of me. I am an overworked professional, an overtired mother, a part-time wife, and a fair-weather friend."

Is that you? Without a vision of what is most important, everything becomes a priority. Everything gets a yes because you have no grid to help you say no. Where there is no vision, life gets out of control, remember?

This is not a new problem. In Titus 2 the apostle Paul encouraged older, more experienced women to step forward and help the younger, less mature women learn how to "be sensible" (Titus 2:5). Even first-century women had trouble with priorities and saying no. So Paul exhorted mature women to build for these younger women a wise decision-making grid that includes loving their husbands (being a helper), loving their children (nurturing a healthy, godly next generation), being sensible (about what you can and should not do), and making a good home "so that the word of God will not be dishonored" (Titus 2:5).

A real woman takes her primary cues in life from the Word of God. This is where she discerns right from wrong, least important from most important, and what's crucial from what's merely optional. But even more importantly, she is convinced that if she dishonors God's Word with her choices, in the end her life will be the real casualty for it. She will miss out on the best in life and often not realize it until it's too late.

Years ago Barbara Bush, the wife of the first President Bush, was invited to give the commencement address at the all-female Wellesley College. Her acceptance unfortunately stirred up a furor. The modern Wellesley girls could not imagine what Mrs. Bush could offer them. She was clearly too old, too traditional, and too yesterday to have anything relevant to say to them. The first lady didn't flinch. Drawing on experience, proven wisdom, and a big-picture perspective of life, she spoke to the students about making wise choices. Here's part of what she had to say: "The . . . choice that must not be missed [as a woman] is to cherish your human connections; your relationships with family and friends. . . . At the end of your life, you will never regret not having passed one more test, not winning one more verdict or not closing one more deal. You will regret time not spent with a husband, a child, a friend or a parent."[7]

Real womanhood is about choosing wisely.

Lives Courageously

Any woman who wants to be a New Eve will find more than her share of roadblocks and challenges. All through life there will be those gut-wrenching crossroads where something prized, desired, or worked for comes up against the greater callings God has for your life. In such moments the call of obedience faces off with personal ambition, long-held dreams, or intense desires.

I remember when my daughter Elizabeth gained admittance to the prestigious London School of Economics for graduate study. It was a dream come true. What an asset this was going to be for her career and future! There was just one problem. She was in the first throes of love with a young man already set in his career in the States. Elizabeth knew two years of graduate study in England would put an enormous strain on their budding relationship.

So what to do in a situation like that? Pray? Yes. Seek counsel? Yes. Try and make both work? Yes. But in the end it came down to making a choice. And what does Scripture say is more important: a career or a lifelong companion? Elizabeth knew the answer. Faced with this life-altering choice, she courageously postponed her graduate-school dreams and chose to deepen her relationship with Brent. In doing so, she sacrificed a certain status in the process, along with greater career opportunities. It was a defining moment. But it was vision—a biblical vision of life and womanhood—that made the difference. Today Elizabeth and Brent are happily married and are the proud parents of my first two grandchildren, Drew and Maggie. Better still, she has no regrets.

Courageously following God in the crossroads of life may or may not put limits on how far your career can go, the experiences you could have had, the skills you could have developed, the fame you could have achieved, or the money you could have earned. But one thing is sure. By following a vision of biblical womanhood, you will get in the end what none of these other things could have provided by themselves: deep fulfillment and purpose as a woman who has courageously stayed true to her callings.

Danielle Crittenden tells the following personal story about trying to have too much too soon and missing the best:

> At a recent party, a highly respected academic and author approached me. She knew I was writing a book about women and, having an inkling of my views, warned me not to romanticize the past too much. "I was there," she said, recalling her days in the early 1960s as a young professor struggling to earn distinction. She told

me that her husband, also a professor, wrote a book at the time that won a much-coveted literary prize. She received a note of congratulations from her own college that read, "How nice [your husband] has someone as intelligent as you to talk to over breakfast." She bristled as she recalled this letter, still incensed by its patronizing tone. "That's what it was like back then," she cautioned me. We moved on to different topics, and she began telling me about her daughter, now in her thirties and also an author, who was unmarried. The woman said that she was longing for her daughter to marry and have children, although of course she respected the younger woman's choices. I began to laugh, and said, "Don't you see what you're telling me? You had to put up with a certain amount of professional disrespect and prejudice, like that letter, but you got everything else— children, a husband who is still devoted to you, and, in the end, enormous professional success, albeit success that took longer than it might have [she had spent time away from academia to raise her kids]. Today, women like me and your daughter take for granted the professional respect you craved, but we can no longer expect marriage, stability, and children when we want them. Who is the bigger loser?"[8]

Expects God's Greater Reward

All choices promise reward. That's just their nature. We choose one option over another because we weigh the potential rewards (outcomes) of each and decide which we like best. For instance, imagine you are a college student and tomorrow you have final exams. What choice will you make tonight? You can go out with the girls and have fun, or you can find a quiet corner and study. Both choices promise reward, and both deliver. Choose to go out, and you are rewarded with good times; choose instead to study, and you are rewarded with a good grade that gets you a step closer to graduation and a good job. In the long run which is the greater reward?

Or how about a harder example? Imagine you live in Honduras. You're married, and though you've tried for years, you are unable to have children. No amount of prayer has changed that. Then a social worker comes to your door. She says there is an infant at the hospital—a malnourished boy who is six months old and weighs only eight pounds. He was born to an eleven-year-old indigent girl who had been raped by a seventy-two-year-old man. Shock and anger rise on your face, and then the social worker asks if the baby can come live with you so that it can die in a loving home. "There is no hope that he will survive," she says.

That's the situation Vera Grafals once faced. She longed to have kids, and in fact, God had been speaking to her about turning that longing toward needy children, but this seemed like too much. "Here I've always wanted a baby," she said, reflecting back, "and suddenly God is asking if He can give me a baby to die in my arms!" It was a hard decision, but Vera knew God had been preparing her. So she took the boy into her home.

She had been told what to expect, but still it was hard watching the baby. He didn't move, talk, or even look around. He merely lay on his back, staring blankly. The lack of nourishment in his earliest weeks had likely damaged his brain, the doctors said, and would be the cause of his early death. Vera tried hard not to think of these things as she cuddled and fed him. She decided to name him Samuel—the name she had always wanted to give a boy. She sang to Samuel, loved him, and waited for him to die.

After a few days, however, changes happened. He began to stir to life. His dark eyes began to focus and show signs of recognition and understanding. Was little Samuel trying to beat the odds? But exactly as hope dawned for Samuel, Vera discovered she had breast cancer. To get the medical treatment she needed, she and her husband, Wally, would have to move to America. Suddenly, the needy little boy in her care was mixed in with her own desperate situation. A decision had to be made. Taking Samuel to America would mean officially adopting him and taking ownership of the inevitable expenses and hardships that come with caring for a special-needs child. Could Vera and her husband handle that at a time when her own life was in danger? Again she was faced with a difficult choice, and again she followed God's leading in her heart. She and Wally adopted Samuel, boarded a plane, and came to America, hoping to find life for both mother and child.

That was ten years ago. Today Samuel is a charming, perfectly normal boy, and Vera is cancer free and serving God through her gifts of compassion and service to children. But Vera's story didn't start with her knowing the end. It started when she made a series of difficult choices, trusting God's leading in her life. The potential downside of each decision was clear, but by faith she moved forward, expecting God's greater reward for choices that had no guarantees on the front end.

Hebrews 11:6 says, "Without faith it is impossible to please Him, for he who comes to God must believe that He is, and that He is a rewarder of those who seek Him." Faith applies to all of life's decisions. But the best faith is faith that believes God will reward those who believe His word with far more than this world can give. Ask Vera Grafals.

Conclusion

All this brings us to a second bold move for any New Eve wanting to live a life that honors God while managing the challenges and opportunities of the twenty-first century. Here it is:

Adopt a biblical definition of womanhood.

Doing so is crucial to vision, and vision is crucial to life. Hopefully, I've gotten you started with your vision by the definition of authentic womanhood set forth in this chapter. But here's the bottom line: as a woman, you cannot become what you cannot define. There will be pain, disappointment, dead ends, and years of undoing, redoing, or catching up on what was neglected or left out if you cannot see and envision where you are going.

The New Eve knows a better way. She has entrusted her life to God and to a biblical vision of womanhood that she believes will prove itself as the years roll by. Mary said it best: "May it be done to me according to your word" (Luke 1:38).

7

The Seasons of a Woman's Life (Part 1)

We have been seeking to construct a lifestyle that works for you as a Christian woman, one that is both true to the Bible and relevant to the modern world you live in. Thus far I have offered two bold moves to that end. First, a New Eve lives from the inside out. Second, she adopts a biblical definition of womanhood and lets that vision guide her life forward. Now here and in chapter 8, I want to discuss a third bold move. Simply put, a New Eve will . . .

Embrace a big-picture perspective on life.

In Ecclesiastes 3:1 Solomon offers this succinct bit of wisdom: "There is an appointed time for everything. And there is a time for every event under heaven." In other words, there are *seasons in life*. And each season naturally carries with it certain unique characteristics, themes, and priorities.

The wise woman will not only understand her current season of life but will also make the appropriate lifestyle choices to go with it. This in turn helps her to build and successfully unleash the next season. The key is not to get so caught up in personal wants and worldly ambitions that you neglect catching the seasonal winds essential to attaining the better life God wants to give you (Deut. 30:15–19; John 10:10b).

Unfortunately, this is what a growing number of women do, especially younger women. *Right now* becomes all they see. Never mind that some aspirations and desires are more suitable to one season than another. They mistakenly believe they can have anything anytime.

Take Evelyn, for example. Sharp and highly educated, she was crystal clear about what she wanted in a career: status, exciting assignments, financial security, and the freedom to make her own choices. The international law firm that hired her offered exactly that kind of future but at a price: long, hard work hours; 24/7 availability; being "dumped on" regularly by senior partners of the firm; and constant deadlines. It was the price of moving up. And in time Evelyn did.

She made junior partner by age twenty-seven and senior partner at thirty-eight. It was a thrilling ride that took everything she had, but it also delivered the future she once dreamed about.

Well . . . almost.

In her late twenties Evelyn became more and more aware of the men in her life. Actually, the lack of them. She had enjoyed a serious relationship the first year out of law school, but that failed shortly after she joined the firm. After that there was a long drought. At thirty-six she fell in love with one of her partners. After a year-long relationship they married. Two wonderful, fun-filled years followed. But then Evelyn turned forty, and it hit her: she wanted a child. So did her husband, Jim. The only problem was they soon found that Evelyn's aging ovaries and lack of eggs had put this now driving obsession out of reach. Even after spending tens of thousands of dollars on every kind of medical procedure possible, the answer always came back the same: no. To everything there is a season. Sadly, Evelyn had missed hers.

Many young women today often have an unconscious defiance to the reality that God has appointed specific seasons for best addressing certain life concerns. They also possess a misplaced optimism that they can catch up later on anything they leave out now. It's crushing when they realize they can't.

Research tells us that 85 percent of college women agree with the statement that "being married is important to me."[1] But then these same young women put off marriage during the very season when there is the best opportunity for finding it. They pursue careers and personal freedom instead. The thinking behind these decisions, of course, is the confidence that they can settle down with a man later on. But when later on arrives, what they may discover is that well-established habits plus the lack of eligible males have left them either alone or hard to live with.

Research also tells us that "89% of young, high-achieving women believe that they will be able to get pregnant in their 40s."[2] But again, the truth is, by that time they have already missed out on their primary childbearing season—ages twenty to thirty. After forty they have at best only a 5 percent chance of pregnancy. And that typically comes only with costly, difficult, drawn-out medical intervention.

So what to do? In exploring the lives of many of today's most successful women, Sylvia Ann Hewlett summed up all she learned about these women and their life choices. She offered young women the following practical advice to help them avoid deep regret in the second half of their lives.

- Figure out what you want your life to look like at age forty-five, both personally and professionally; then live your life to that end.
- Give urgent priority to finding a life partner. This project is extremely time-sensitive and deserves your special attention in your twenties.
- Have your first child before you are thirty-five.
- Choose a career that will give you both the gift of time and the help you need to achieve a work/life balance.
- Avoid professions with rigid career trajectories.[3]

Some women may be quick to react to and speak out against these suggestions as regressive for women. But a woman who keeps in mind the big picture of life will take the time to explore the wisdom of Hewlett's advice. Freedoms, opportunities, and responsibilities all ebb and flow according to the rhythms of specific seasons God has designed for life. A wise woman will choose to flow *with* these seasons, not against them. She will seek to discern what each season offers and requires of her; then she will adjust and focus her life to make the most of it. She knows if she does this, it will also help launch a successful next season rather than undercut it with poor choices.

I believe there are typically ten seasons of life. Individually and collectively, they present a balanced and coordinated bigger picture of life that every woman would be wise to keep in mind.

{	1 Single Adult	}	{	2 Single and Engaged	}	{	3 Newly Married No Children	}
{	4 Married with Preschoolers	}	{	5 Married with Grade- Schoolers	}	{	6 Married, Young-Adult Children	}
{	7 Married, Empty Nester	} {	8 Married In-Law, Grandparent	} {	9 Late-in-Life Widow	} {	10 Glorified Saint	}

As you look over these ten seasons of life, let me point out that beginning with season 3, divorce or the untimely death of a spouse can greatly alter the dynamics of the seasons that follow. So can remaining single and never marrying or finding oneself unable to have children. We will speak to some of these experiences in the next chapter. For now I'll address the standard flow of life through the first five seasons of a woman's life and offer guidance for living wisely through each unfolding season.

Single Adult

In the movie *The Terminal* Tom Hanks portrays Viktor Navorski, an eastern European who is forced to live in the JFK airport because while he was flying over the Atlantic, his home country ceased to exist through a military coup. He deplanes only to find that his visa is void and his money worthless. Worse still, Viktor is not permitted to exit the terminal and enter America, nor is he able to return home. He's stranded between destinations because he doesn't belong anywhere.

Single adulthood can feel a lot like that. You've left childhood behind, but without marriage and children your adulthood probably feels incomplete. Your life is lived at an interchange. People come and go. Some befriend you. Others date you. But as time goes on, many also leave you and move on with their lives. And there you sit like Viktor, feeling as if you don't belong anywhere or to anyone.

God invites you to see things differently. From His perspective your single years are alive with opportunity. The apostle Paul said in 1 Corinthians 7:32–35 that single people are in some ways actually better able to focus on the things of God. Rather than wastefully living for the moment, the wise single woman will adopt this better perspective and focus on the key priorities unique to this season of life.

First is character development. What sort of woman do you want to become? It's *the* question in this season of life. What you decide here and act on will either serve or shackle you for seasons to come. Please hear that. Character is the ground floor of life. Who you are will always be more important than what you do. *Always.*

In 1 Timothy 4:12 Paul said, "Let no one look down on your youthfulness, but rather in speech, conduct, love, faith and purity, show yourself an example of those who believe." Solomon's proverbs flesh out these general character traits with more specifics. Truth telling, generosity, sexual restraint, accountability, and a strong work ethic are only some of the items discussed in this wisdom lit-

SINGLE ADULT

Wise Moves

- Character development
- Skill and career development
- Spiritual life development and Kingdom service
- Solid understanding of the opposite sex

Key Verse:
1 Timothy 4:12

erature. The point is that in your single years you have a unique opportunity to build your character rather than take on the harder work of *re*building it as some women have to do in later seasons. No one can choose your character for you. Character is intensely personal work. And it is work! As the historian James Froude once said, "You cannot dream yourself into a character; you must hammer and forge yourself one."[4]

So let me ask again: What kind of woman do you aspire and strive to be? Can you name the traits you want people to discuss when they speak about you behind your back? Know this: the better your character, the better your life. And as a single woman, you have lots of discretionary time to hammer it out.

Second, as a single woman, you should spend your time developing your career abilities. Somehow Christianity has been tagged as anticareer in regard to women, but the fact is, every Christian woman should maximize her career potential. After all, it is God Himself who gave you that potential, and you never know how He might choose to use you. Holding back your abilities is like stopping yourself at the doorway to the arena in which you were born to perform. Let yourself go! Run free and hard into all the great things you can do and achieve. Even as I write, my single daughter Rebekah is serving as a teacher in Rwanda with internationals and children of the genocide. The skills she has developed during her singleness make this doable. Many of the skills and abilities you develop as a single will come back and bless you and others again and again in new ways in the following seasons. You may be surprised at the people and the opportunities that come calling. So give yourself to skill development.

I strongly suggest you use a number of the wonderful personality and vocational testing profiles available to help you identify both who you are and the gifts and talents you possess. Some I have used are www.strengthfinder.com from the

Gallup organization, www.aimstesting.org (Aptitude Inventory Measurement Services), and www.youruniquedesign.com. Each of these offers tremendous help in knowing yourself, your strengths, and what settings those strengths are best released in. Your single years, from a personality and abilities perspective, are the best time to discover who you are, who you're *not* (sometimes this is even more important than knowing who you are), and what kinds of things make you come alive.

Third, you have more time now than ever to focus on your spiritual life. There are incredible spiritual opportunities for you to explore for growth and maturity as a believer in Christ. Don't cram your schedule full of empty busyness. Sure, you should enjoy life. See places, do things, go though doors that open only once. But put God at the center of it all. Link up with other passionate Christians. Study God's Word together. Develop a consistent time with God alone. Use your gifts in serving others and advancing His kingdom. Make the most of your time and be watchful for the roles you can play in God's unfolding drama.

Finally, your single years are the right time to investigate that strange male creature to whom you are drawn. I strongly recommend you read good books that dissect the male personality, his needs, and his slant on life. Master the insights you find there. Become male smart and live from this informed perspective. Get past the stereotypes and the caricatures and find out what really makes a man tick. Learn what authentic manhood is and discover how to judge a man by it. Know what to look for in a man before you find one of them bowed before you with a ring in his hand and a glint in his eye. Remember this: the best way to find a good man and keep him is to become a good woman (1 Tim. 4:12).

Single and Engaged

Love. There's nothing like it, especially in this season of life when it glows red-hot. Life is now about "togetherness." You and _____. It's a time consumed with drawing close. And that's where you need to be careful. Feelings often dominate this time. And though there is nothing wrong with that, it's important to realize that true closeness and close feelings are not necessarily the same thing.

Real closeness comes about only when two people value and embrace the same things. As the psalmist expressed thousands of years ago in Psalm 133:1–3, "Behold, how good and how pleasant it is for brothers to dwell together in unity! . . . for there the LORD commanded the blessing—life forever." What applies to brothers also applies to marriage partners. Unity is life-giving. No two people can live together in harmony very long if the deeper chords of values and beliefs are out of sync. And that is where the danger is. The intense but superficial feelings a couple have for one another during their engagement can often block them from exploring and dealing with these very real issues.

For instance, are both of you in sync with God's purposes for your marriage? That's certainly one of those deeper chords. When I ask this question, it often draws a blank stare from engaged couples. God's purposes?

> **SINGLE AND ENGAGED**
>
> ## *Wise Moves*
>
> - Embrace God's purposes for marriage.
> - Participate in a quality premarital program that addresses marriage roles, expectations, differences, values, money, and conflict resolution.
> - Know the strengths and weaknesses of each other's personality.
>
> *Key Verse:*
> *2 Corinthians 6:14*

Remember, in Genesis God called the man and woman together for three specific reasons: for deep companionship, for raising healthy children, and for advancing His kingdom. To be married before God means forging a covenant together for aggressively pursuing these priorities and ordering life around them.

Of course, to do this requires a certain level of spiritual maturity and spiritual compatibility between you and your fiancé. That being the case, let me ask another deeper-chord question essential to your relationship. Are you both Christians? If you are and he's not, the Bible warns you *not* to move forward in this relationship. "Do not be bound together with unbelievers," 2 Corinthians 6:14 says. Why the hard line? Because the deepest language of marriage is spiritual language. Nothing draws a couple closer and keeps them closer than a shared spiritual life. Therefore, be careful not to overlook or whitewash this vital area during your engagement. Be honest and ask tough questions. A broken engagement now is far better than a broken marriage later. On the other hand, laying a common spiritual foundation will be the single most important thing you can do for your marriage. It will undergird every other season to come.

Be sure that you also take advantage of well-designed premarital preparation. See if a class or training program is offered at your church. If not, find one. And if all else fails, look for one you can work through on video or on the Internet. It would be wise to ask an older, successful married couple to join you in this video experience. Interact with them about the information presented.

The point is: don't enter marriage unprepared! Most marriages that fail today fail within the first five years. On the other hand, research has shown that good premarital training virtually guarantees that this will not be the case for you. Make sure your premarital preparation includes large amounts of discussion, interaction, and practical helps over such vital topics as money, values, conflict resolution, marriage roles, marriage expectations, and sex. It would also be extremely helpful if this time included personality testing as well. Know this: personalities never change. You can rub off some of the rough spots, but basically, you are who you are. So the more you can know about each other's core personality—the strengths, the weaknesses, the pluses, the minuses, the needs of that personality, the language of that personality, and so on—the better.

Finally, read a few good-quality books on marriage. Two classics I highly recommend are Willard Harley's *His Needs, Her Needs* and Gary Chapman's *The Five Love Languages*.

If all of this makes marriage sound like serious business, it is. The majority of the happiness you will experience in life as a woman will come from it. That's the wonderful upside. So don't ignore learning about marriage even as you enjoy this high-intensity season of love.

Newly Married/No Children

Now you've arrived, right? Actually, you've just begun. You've trained, studied, sought advice, and looked deeply into the vital issues of marriage, and now the first thing you need to do is *keep on* doing these things. Keep reading. Every year make it a point to take a class on an aspect of marriage. Go as a couple to a marriage conference. Seek wise counsel when conflicts arise. This is also a great time for your husband to go through one of my Men's Fraternity curricula, such as *Winning at Work and Home* or *The Quest for Authentic Manhood* (www.mensfraternity.com). Like professional athletes, keep up your training regimen at all times. Keep investing.

Today 43 percent of all first-time marriages end in divorce. That sobering statistic means you will have to take your marriage much more seriously than much of the world does.

Maybe even more seriously than your parents did. Seek third-party support for your young marriage. Find a couple who has been in the marriage game longer than you. Go to this husband and wife for advice. Open your life. Drain tension. Get wisdom. Make them your life coaches. Let them peer in through the windows to your soul. Let them ask hard questions. It will feel invasive at first, but windowless lives almost always have trouble. Don't close yourself off from the help available.

It's also vital to erect some firm financial disciplines early in your marriage to which both of you agree and adhere. You'll probably both be working. This season invites that. So develop your abilities and gain confidence and experience in a career path. Establish yourself. Remember, what you gain from work now can be leveraged in other seasons of life as something to fall back on or as something with which to open new doors. So make the most of it.

But be careful with the money you make as a couple. A double income is seductive. You can overbuy, overextend, and destabilize your marriage. You can quickly become enslaved to financial obligations and commitments (car payments, mortgages, and loans) that demand you work even during seasons when you long to be home. A radical and wise step would be to live on one income from the start. My wife and I did that. Every month we put her entire teacher's salary into savings.

**NEWLY MARRIED
WITH NO CHILDREN**

Wise Moves

- Continue expanding your marriage skills.
- Set clear financial boundaries.
- Identify and develop common fun activities.
- Make the most of your career opportunities.

*Key Verse:
Ephesians 5:31*

We knew when kids came along, she would want to stay home with them while they were young. So we purposely lived a one-income lifestyle from the beginning. We bought used cars and limited our purchases.

Besides, what we really desired in this opening season of our marriage was not stuff but rich experiences together. *Fun.* Some of the money we saved during this time gave us this opportunity in a big way. After a year of disciplined living, we made a memory most couples only dream about for their retirement. We packed our bags and took off to Europe and the Middle East. We rode camels to the pyramids, sailed down the Nile under moonlight, scampered up the Eiffel Tower like teenagers, stood on the Mount of Olives overlooking Jerusalem, and walked the shores of Galilee. That was nearly forty years ago, and we haven't stopped talking about it yet. It created in both of us a love of travel that has now become our common fun. As for the new car we didn't buy in those early days, well, we haven't missed it once.

Finally, get involved together in a local church. Build a Christian community around you. Research shows that couples who attend church together on a regular basis are between 35 and 50 percent less likely than all other Americans, including infrequent churchgoers, to get a divorce.[5]

Married with Preschoolers

I once saw a bumper sticker that said, "My children saved me from toxic self-absorption." There's a lot of truth in that. If ever there was a season of life that is not about you, this is it. Your little ones require major-league attention. They are desperate for face time with you. Lots of it.

I once read a story about a young third-grader named Timmy who was having trouble at school. Timmy's mother was called in to discuss his poor performance. She heard about his reading problems and his struggles with math. Then the teacher asked, "Why does Timmy always say, 'Love is slow'?" Timmy's mother suddenly began to sob. She knew. She then explained about her demanding job and the long hours she had to give to it. To get to work on time in the morning, she had to constantly push Timmy along. Then at night after a long day, she had to rush back home to cook dinner, clean up, and get to bed. The whole time she was pressing Timmy to finish his homework, pick up his toys, take a bath, and so on. "I find myself constantly saying to him, 'Timmy, you are so slow!'"

For any child, love is slow. You simply cannot properly nurture the next generation without large amounts of time and focused attention. That's particularly true for children five years of age and younger. But for whatever reasons, today it's very hard for many young mothers to hear that.

In a recent landmark study conducted by Dartmouth Medical School, researchers discovered that the way a child's brain wires itself, neurologically speaking, is determined *after* birth by the care and attention he or she receives. *Love* shapes a child's brain! Love helps a child's brain connect itself together in a healthy way. The Dartmouth study also found that if a child is neglected and the love he or she needs falls short, these same neurological connectors actually *mis*connect, creating emotional and intellectual deficits in the brain that can last a lifetime.[6]

MARRIED WITH PRESCHOOLERS

Wise Moves

- Be there for your children.
- Keep time for your marriage.
- Avoid major debt.
- Carefully evaluate your career with your husband.

Key Verse: Titus 2:4–5

New sociological data backs up these findings. It shows that as the economy and standard of living in America has skyrocketed in the past thirty years, so has the rate of mental disorders and emotional problems among children.[7] Busy, career-minded parents, absent emotionally or physically, breed troubled kids. It's an epidemic money doesn't fix. That's the short of it. Nothing is more indispensable to a young child than large amounts of time and attention from a loving mother and father. Nothing.

Your spouse needs you too in this season of life. Frankly, a lot of the things that were fun when you first married—spontaneity, freedom, and extra money—are simply gone now, banished by a teetering pile of diapers, sleepless nights, calls for "Watch me," and growing pains. This is a major marriage adjustment time.

That being said, you *must* keep time for your spouse. This will not be easy. Early-childhood parenting is exhausting, but you cannot allow it to eclipse your marriage. The best survival remedy I know is the one Sherard and I practiced for years in this season of our lives: we took quarterly getaways together. These can do what the frenzy of everyday life at this stage cannot do: provide you with some much-needed downtime when you can rest and focus on one another. You may not have a lot of money for this, but a special overnighter (or more) once every three months will serve as an oasis of refreshment for you and your husband to talk, reflect, plan, play, and romance. And don't call home either. Make it a clean break. The kids will be OK. Trust me.

You'll also need to be careful with your finances. Yes, this is a theme for every season of life. But here it raises a huge question: Will you continue to work? Full-time? Part-time? What about scaling back? Is that possible? Or will you be transitioning at this point from two incomes to one? This can be a time of courageous faith or real tension, especially if you're conflicted about whether you should or can stay at home while the kids are young. But no matter what you decide, it needs to be a *team* decision between you and your husband that's made after careful consideration of God's Word, your unique situation, and what's best for your children.

Married with Grade-Schoolers

This is an odd time for you as a woman. In some ways you feel you're able to ratchet down your commitment level. No more diapers. You're sleeping again. The kids can bathe and dress themselves just fine. You breathe a little easier.

Or do you?

The fact is, you might find yourself ramping up your efforts as never before. You run the kids from school to soccer to baseball to tutoring to the overnighter at the Joneses' place. You do parties, graduations, and school plays. If you're like my wife when our kids were in school, all this adds up to twenty-five thousand miles a year on the minivan. That's enough to circle the earth!

During this season many moms who are working begin to feel, as never before, that they're missing special moments in their children's lives. There's simply not enough time. Other mothers begin to entertain the idea of going back to work as their children grow older. But how much work? The truth is, a career mixes hard with the needs of a husband and school-age kids. There are no easy answers or formulas. Therefore, it is important in this season constantly to assess the work-home balance. Am I being a helper to my husband? Does he feel my support? My love? Are my children getting the love and attention they need from me? Will they feel I was there for them?

Perhaps the best and easiest way to get answers to these questions is to ask your family directly. If you do this in a sincere and humble way, you'll probably get honest feedback. From their input you can then choose to adjust or stay the course.

Financially, both income and expenses will probably keep rising in this season. You'll find it's extremely easy to spend more money than you make and nearly impossible to save too much. It was at this time that Sherard and I decided to impose the 10-10-80 rule. That is, save 10 percent, give away 10 percent, and spend the rest (avoiding major debt). If that sounds like a simple financial plan, it was. But at times it was also agonizingly hard to implement. We watched friends buy and do things that were within the reach of our credit cards. But we resisted using them. We drove preowned cars until there was no life left in them. Many of the upgrades on our home, we did ourselves. It wasn't that we lived as Spartans. Far from it. We enjoyed life. But it was a financially disciplined life.

We began to see the real fruit of our 10-10-80 rule after about seventeen years. That's right—seventeen years! One day I looked at my financial-investment account and saw that I had already put enough money away to send three of my four children to college. I even had a small retirement account too. All because at age twenty-seven Sherard and I made some firm financial choices that were hard at the time. (You might want to start even earlier.) Yes, we missed out on a few things, but over time we gained a whole lot more.

How are you and your husband dealing with your finances

MARRIED WITH GRADE-SCHOOLERS

Wise Moves

- Watch your pace. If you are working, assess how it is impacting your family.
- Get serious about saving for college and retirement.
- Adjust your parenting according to each child's particular personality and gifts.
- Explore Kingdom work you can invest your abilities in.

Key Verse: Proverbs 22:6

in this season of life? If you're wise, you will get serious *now* about saving for college and retirement.

Finally, as your children move through their school years, their unique personalities and talents should become more and more apparent. I cannot stress enough how important it is for you as a parent to both recognize and honor who your child is and what gifts and abilities he or she possesses. Don't overlook or play down talents that seem odd or undesirable to you. Play up your child's gifts! And don't try to make children what they're not. Don't try and make a musician an athlete or push your easygoing kid to be an aggressive goal setter. Let them be themselves, whatever course that takes. Make them feel special because of their gifts.

Proverbs 22:6 says, "Train up a child in the way he should go." A more literal translation would be, "Train up a child according to his bent." It is every parent's job to know and honor this bent. It is also your job to encourage that bent to grow and flourish. In that regard, basic personality and gift testing is crucial for you to have an objective appraisal of your child. The earlier, the better. This becomes very helpful in knowing how to influence your child's life as he or she moves through school, especially through junior high and high school.

Conclusion

This concludes our discussion on the first half of your seasons as a woman. The next chapter will address the other half as well as some exceptions. But as we finish here, don't lose sight of why I am giving you this big-picture perspective of life. It's to help you see "there is a time for every event under heaven" (Eccles. 3:1).

8

The Seasons of a Woman's Life (Part 2)

Some of you may be quick to comment that you don't really fit these general seasons of life I'm describing. For you, life is different because of circumstances you could not control or difficulties you helped create. My good friend Sandy Bone is one who knows that the expected seasons of life can sometimes get off track. Early in her fifties Sandy had her life turned upside down. After twenty-six years of marriage and raising two children, Sandy's husband was tragically killed in an automobile accident. Suddenly, the flow of life Sandy had long experienced made a hard U-turn into an unexpected new life: single again. Thrown into this strange new season, Sandy needed a game plan. The path that once seemed straight and simple was now crowded with new forks and bends.

Tragedy can do that. It can rip you from your comfort zone and set you down hard in a place where you're not sure what to do next. Divorce can do this too. So can infertility, remaining unmarried, or marrying a man who already has kids. In these and other cases, the more typical and sequential seasons of a woman's life get scrambled, rearranged, or even repeated. So what do you do? How do you find your footing and make wise moves when the scenery of your life takes on an out-of-the-ordinary color?

You can start the process of discovering your new ground rules by blending two of the common seasons of life into a new, hybrid category that best describes your situation. Here's what I mean. First, select from the ten seasons I listed for you in chapter 7 the two that best describe your life now. For instance, if you have three grade-school children but are recently divorced, then the two seasons that best align themselves with where you are now would be "Single" and "Married with Grade-Schoolers."

Next, select from these two seasons the wise moves in each that best apply to your particular situation. By combining these moves, you will find wisdom and direction for your new, hybrid season: "Single with Grade-Schoolers." In such a case your wise moves for this blended season might look something like what is on the following page.

You can do this with any exception to the ten standard seasons. Did you marry a man with young-adult children? Then you are "Newly Married with Young-Adult Children." Are you a young mom who just got engaged? Then you are "Single and Engaged with Preschoolers." Are you married, childless, and middle-aged? Then you are "Married without Children," but you have common ground with an "Empty Nester." The point is, by blending any two of the more common seasons of life, you can create a wise course for your life.

This is what Sandy had to do. The tragic car accident converted her from a "Married Empty Nester" to a "Single Empty

SINGLE ADULT

Wise Moves

- Character development
- Skill and career development
- Spiritual life development and Kingdom service
- Solid understanding of the opposite sex

MARRIED WITH GRADE-SCHOOLERS

Wise Moves

- Watch your pace. If you are working, assess how it is impacting your family.
- Get serious about saving for college and retirement.
- Adjust your parenting according to each child's particular personality and gifts.
- Explore Kingdom work you can invest your abilities in.

SINGLE WITH GRADE-SCHOOLERS

Wise Moves

- Skill and career development
- Watch your pace and how work is impacting your kids.
- Spiritual life development; your Kingdom service is your *kids.*
- Parent each child uniquely.
- Solid understanding of the opposite sex

Nester." Like most singles, she needed a job. But which? Sandy had a college degree in teaching, but she had never used those skills except for a brief time when she led the women's ministry at our church. The idea of having to support herself was terrifying. Initially she opened her home to international students to help offset the rent and utilities. She also worked at Dillards for $8.50 an hour. As humbling as this was, Sandy knew it was God's way of stretching her character in new and unexpected ways. "This is what I had to keep telling myself," she says with a smile. In this kind of situation, a woman must choose between faith and despair. Sandy chose faith.

Through it all her Christian friends were a great source of encouragement. "I couldn't have made it without them. They were incredible." Her adult children offered their support too, but they could go only so far. They needed their space and the opportunity to live their own lives. Just because Sandy was single again did not mean she could use her situation to bond with them like before. Sandy understood this, but it also meant she felt really alone.

After a year of merely making ends meet, Sandy knew it was time to do something more meaningful with her life. As we discussed earlier, singles need to focus on ability and career development, while empty nesters need new work after kids in which to invest their lives. Being both single and an empty nester, Sandy began to investigate where her skills and interests could best be used. One thing kept surfacing: she liked to help people who were hurting. This realization led her to take "the wildest, riskiest leap of my life."

She enrolled in graduate school to become a professional counselor. "I was older than all my professors and even the dean of the college. I had to work really, really hard. I cried more in my statistics classes than at any other time in my life. But it became more and more evident that God was with me, sustaining me, empowering me. It was amazing what He did for me." We who watched were also amazed—amazed at God and this wonderful woman He was blessing.

At age fifty-eight, after three and one-half years of graduate studies and another three and one-half years of residency work, Sandy took her national boards and became a licensed counselor. Her life and faith heroics set an example for all of us who watched her during those years. And God rewarded her for it too, not only with a good job but also with a new husband! I had the privilege of marrying Gayle and Sandy, and it was probably the most gratifying wedding I have ever performed. Before me was a real New Eve whose bold, courageous faith God had rewarded with a better life. I recently asked Sandy, now sixty-five, how things were going. "I'm at the happiest, most exciting time of my life," she replied. I wasn't a bit surprised.

Of course, it's one thing for life circumstances to scramble your seasons. It's another thing for you to do it to yourself by engaging in a reckless live-in relationship or ignoring God's callings in favor of career ambitions and material things. These choices fly in the face of the natural flow of a woman's life, and all come with a high price tag attached. As the old saying goes, "You can't fool Mother Nature." When you try, you're the one who gets fooled. It's so much better to go with the seasonal currents of life and maximize their opportunities than it is to fight against that flow and pay heavy penalties. The more you can see and appreciate this bigger picture of life, the better you'll be able to see your way to the good life. Now let's finish outlining the final five seasons of a woman's life.

Married with Young-Adult Children

You've taken your kids through "Ready" and "Set," now it's time for *"Go!"* Like it or not, your older teenage children increasingly need their own space. As emerging adults, they are in the serious business of defining their own lives, and they must do this more and more without you. This means you must transition from your role as chief caregiver, guardian, and standard bearer to one that more resembles that of a friend and occasional consultant. This is difficult for most moms. It's natural to want to maintain a close, protective orbit around your kids' lives, but doing so will do more harm than good. You'll exhaust everyone if you try to preserve unmodified that original bond you had with your kids. Yes, they need a mother for life, but what they don't need is *mothering* for life. That can actually harm your kids—especially sons.

When a mom refuses to let go of her son but instead overnurtures and overmothers him, one of two bad things may happen. First, she may inadvertently train her son to fear closeness with a woman. That's because closeness to Mom brought with it her control and smothering love. Therefore, for his masculinity and sense of autonomy to survive, the son must constantly push his mother away and rebel against her excessive involvement. But in doing so, he also learns at this impressionable age to fear *all* feminine love as a threat to self. Later as adults, men like this can successfully relate only to women they can dominate. No giving

MARRIED WITH YOUNG-ADULT CHILDREN

Wise Moves

- Change parenting style to release children into adulthood.

- Establish a long-range financial plan.

- Back to work?

- Find Kingdom work that excites you and utilizes your skill set.

- Make time for special marriage getaways.

Key Verse: Proverbs 31:10–27

in. No compromise. No getting too close. No talking back. Just do as I say. This is how such men feel safe with women. It's a survivalist tactic they learned at home in their relationship with Mom.

Second, a mother who bonds too deeply with her son may breed an overly feminized man. Rather than fight against his mother's control, this son instead wholeheartedly embraces it and lets it rob him of his emerging manhood. For that, he will remain a boy emotionally even as he grows into a man physically. Instead of leading and caring for the women in his life, he will instead look to them to do these things for him—exactly as Mom did. Today America is full of such men. They are soft, passive, noninitiating males who have lost the will to be men because they yielded to moms who loved and cared too much to let them grow up. The wise mother understands that her God-given mandate is to prepare her children for autonomous living. Family relationships are never meant to be broken, but the emotional umbilical cord tying mother and child tightly together has to be cut in this season of life.

Then there's work. If you have been a stay-at-home mom, now might be the time for you to consider reengaging your career either part-time or full-time. With your children stretching toward newfound autonomy, this season provides the opportunity to think beyond childrearing. You've been away from the workplace for a while, and no doubt your first steps will feel tentative and untrained, but courage and diligence can move you forward again. You might think of the Proverbs 31 woman in this context. She certainly cared for her family's needs, but she was also industrious (as you can be) in other spheres as well. In verses 10–27 we read of her daily routine.

An excellent wife, who can find?
For her worth is far above jewels.

The heart of her husband trusts in her,
    And he will have no lack of gain.
She does him good and not evil
    All the days of her life.
She looks for wool and flax
    And works with her hands in delight.
She is like merchant ships;
    She brings her food from afar.
She rises also while it is still night
    And gives food to her household
    And portions to her maidens.
She considers a field and buys it;
    From her earnings she plants a vineyard.
She girds herself with strength
    And makes her arms strong.
She senses that her gain is good;
    Her lamp does not go out at night.
She stretches out her hands to the distaff,
    And her hands grasp the spindle.
She extends her hand to the poor,
    And she stretches out her hands to the needy.
She is not afraid of the snow for her household,
    For all her household are clothed with scarlet.
She makes coverings for herself;
    Her clothing is fine linen and purple.
Her husband is known in the gates,
    When he sits among the elders of the land.
She makes linen garments and sells them,
    And supplies belts to the tradesmen.
Strength and dignity are her clothing,
    And she smiles at the future.

She opens her mouth in wisdom,
  And the teaching of kindness is on her tongue.
She looks well to the ways of her household,
  And does not eat the bread of idleness. (emphasis added)

I have a strong sense that this Proverbs 31 woman is in the season of life we are now addressing: "Married with Young-Adult Children." And it is here that she is able to pull off a remarkable balance of being wife and mother while adding things like real-estate developer, fashion designer, salesperson, and Kingdom builder into the mix. You have the chance here to spread your wings as well. With your teenagers preparing to leave home or entering college and with growing needs for extra income and retirement savings, stepping back into part-time or full-time work may be a wise move. This might also start the process of crafting a new vision for the vocational aspect of your life.

On the other hand, maybe you have the financial freedom to forgo a career. For you there is the opportunity to consider instead a new and more expanded phase of Kingdom work. Maybe you will volunteer your skills at church, at a school, at a local faith-based agency, or in a ministry on the other side of the world! Yes, you *can* do that. Mentor young women, tutor struggling students, serve on the board of a nonprofit, do charity fund-raising, help plant a new church, develop a Christian drama team, do financial counseling, work in a recovery program, develop and oversee your church's Web site, work with international students, or lead your own ministry organization. It's your life. Make it an adventure!

This is also the time to enjoy life with your husband in new and exciting ways. For example, in this season Sherard and I decided to sell our house and buy another one we could remodel together for life after the kids are gone. We made it *our* project *for us.* We also took several exotic vacations. Only the two of us. With extra time and with your adult children often consumed with their own agendas, the opportunity is there to step out in new and bold ways. So go for it!

Married Empty Nester

An amazing thing happens when the last kid packs up and leaves the house: you and your husband start dating again. You rediscover the movie theaters and restaurants that mysteriously fell off your map decades ago. You sleep in, eat out, stop over, and drive on and on to wherever the scenic road leads. This is a time for marital revitalization. Or at least it should be! With the kids gone, the opportunity is there to forge new goals and plan new adventures together. Don't miss this opportunity, or you will miss each other.

I remember talking with one empty-nester friend of mine who surprised me with the announcement that he had recently purchased a motorcycle. "It's time to ride!" he bellowed. I laughed as I pictured my friend—a quiet, humble physician— morphing into a wild, carefree biker roaring down the highway. Then I asked, "What did your wife think about your buying a motorcycle?" He paused for a moment and then with a boyish grin said, "She bought one too." Now there's a wise woman. The couple that plays together stays together.

This season is also a time to compose new and exciting individual goals. Really, your career options are wide open now. You can restart your former career and do so with the satisfaction that you've been the mom your children needed. Or you might dare to take up the challenge of an entirely new pursuit. You could try your hand at art, teaching, administration, caregiving, leadership, or even something as bold and meaningful as what Lisa Smith and her husband, Frank, did.

Lisa and Frank had truly arrived. After twenty years of hard work and faithfulness, they had established themselves as pillars in their church, their community, and their workplaces. Best of all, they had succeeded in raising their two sons to follow Christ. As for finances, they had practiced careful stewardship with everything God gave them. Now they were middle-aged and debt free. With a household income well into six figures, they had the freedom to buy the toys they'd always dreamed of—a boat, luxury cars, or a beachside condo—all of these things were real possibilities now that the children were all grown up.

So what did they do? They sold their big house and all their furniture. *All* of it. Time for bigger and better, right? Well, yes. Freshly relieved of all their property, Frank and Lisa drove hundreds of miles north and began seminary, specifically with missions on their minds. After a year of intense preparation, they launched their new careers.

Rather than shuttling off to some corporate hot spot on the coast, they caught a day-long plane ride and took up quarters among the poor in a faraway country I can't mention by name. It's a country that's hostile to all things American. Instead of chatting about stock dividends and fiscal fitness over power lunches with business associates, they chose instead to practice a strange new language in torrid street markets, secret worship services, and ramshackle buses

---

MARRIED EMPTY NESTER

Wise Moves

- Build new ways of connecting with your husband and enjoying life together.
- Reinvent your life!
- Invest more time in Kingdom work that engages your gifts and interests.
- Consider mentoring younger women from your life experiences.

Key Verse:
Titus 2:3–5

that roar down narrow dirt streets. As empty nesters, Frank and Lisa have leveraged their newfound freedom to connect a strange part of the world to the love of Christ.[1]

Of course, you don't have to cross oceans to find Kingdom work. You might not even have to leave your home. Kingdom work is everywhere. As an empty nester, you may need to invite an elderly parent into your home, or you might be called on to support parents financially and emotionally, as I did when my mom was alone and ill late in life. Sure, it was hard at times. To serve my mother in this way was both a privilege and a Christian mandate for Sherard and me (1 Tim. 5:4). And when on a cold Easter morning it fell to me to go into her hospital room and inform her that she had inoperable brain cancer, her words were a vindication of our sacrifices for her. She smiled and said, "Robert, I want you to know how good my life has been these last two years with you and Sherard watching out for me. Thank you."

It's not only elderly parents you can look after and care for in this season of life. Scripture says you are also uniquely positioned to look after the younger women around you who desperately need your wisdom and experience. Titus 2:4–5 exhorts older women to help younger women learn how to live *smart*. "Encourage the young women to love their husbands, to love their children, to be sensible, pure, workers at home, kind, being subject to their own husbands, so that the word of God may not be dishonored." Every new generation of women needs to hear that. It's a challenging message that's best heard from the lips of older women whose life experiences (both good and bad) confirm such wisdom. In this season of life, you can do that!

Several years after a painful divorce, Shirley James was asked by one of the pastors at our church to mentor a young woman. Shirley was skeptical. "I weighed his request against the amount of credibility I thought I had, and it seemed I fell short." But with the encouragement of friends, Shirley took a leap of faith and met a discouraged young woman named Jennifer for lunch.

"We ate and chatted for a while. She told me about her troubled childhood, and I told her about my divorce. As we wrapped up, I felt I needed to be clear about my concerns. I said, 'Well, now you know my story. My marriage failed, and I've got some wounds. Can you really be interested in taking me on as your mentor?' Of course, I expected her to say no. I had prepared for it all week. It was the sort of self-rejection I was used to by now. But then to my amazement Jennifer said yes! When I asked her why she would choose me, she said, 'I feel I can trust you because of your scars. You've been hurt, and you've felt unworthy just like I have, so I know you'll be real with me.'"

Looking back now, Shirley sees that this was when her life really started to turn back in the direction it was always meant to take. "For the first time I began to see that my pain, which I thought was a mark of my failure and uselessness, could actually be used by God to bless others."

Shirley met with Jennifer weekly, talking through the pain, disappointment, and fear each of them had experienced and finding hope in God's promises and principles. Each time they met, Shirley realized more and more that God was healing both of them in the process. In the years that followed, Shirley had the privilege of giving Jennifer away at her wedding and becoming a grandmother (called Nonie) to Jennifer's little girl, Sophie.

As I write, Shirley's daughters have all grown up to be mature Christian women—women who have learned a lot from their mother. Meanwhile, Shirley is changing lives by actively pursuing other young women who are interested in spiritually intimate, honest relationships. Mentoring is a great way to invest your life and advance God's kingdom.

Married, and You're an In-Law and Grandparent!

In this season your family has expanded. And with that expansion you have been given new roles and new responsibilities. There are also new rules to play by.

Some women really struggle here. They have trouble adjusting to the "strangers" their children bring home as mates as well as the new values, new ways of doing things, new schedules, and new identities that come with them. Maybe your daughter has picked up new interests you care little for. Maybe she's going to spend this Christmas with her husband's family and not, as she's always done, with you. Or maybe your son's politics have shifted away from yours. In these situations, it's easy to become the notorious mother-in-law who criticizes, controls, demands, intrudes, violates, and never lets go.

Be careful here. You want to start right and stay right. This is a time for establishing new, healthy boundaries between you and your children's marriages and for building strong, accepting relationships with their spouses. For instance, it blesses a son when *you* reach out to the young woman he's chosen to spend his life with and genuinely embrace her. Best of all is when you present an attitude that says, "How can I support, help, and bless you?" (1 Pet. 3:8–11).

Your grandparent role is vital too. Unfortunately, I never had the opportunity to connect with my grandparents when I was growing up. All but one of them had died by the time I was old enough to be aware of them, and the surviving one, Granny, was a bedridden invalid. So I missed out on experiencing the powerful role my grandparents could play.

My kids were much more blessed. They had grandparents who both loved them and were involved in their lives. And what a difference that made! Their presence has given my children a greater sense of connectedness, shared values, heritage, and legacy, not to mention a bigger perspective on life.

So as a grandmother, your work on your family's behalf is not finished. In new and refreshing ways you can make your life count for your grandchildren's betterment. Slip them a dose of wisdom every chance you get. Wrap it in holiday cakes, birthday cards, and warm words. Be a model of love and encouragement. Tell your grandchildren stories of your life. Lots of them. I will always treasure the memories of my mom mesmerizing my children with tales of growing up in a small Louisiana town: her rides on her pony, Buttermilk; digging up arrowheads in her backyard; her Jewish friends who opened her eyes to the larger world; and the account of Charles Lindbergh landing his plane in a bean field near her home. In everything show your grandchildren how life can finish with strength and dignity. In doing so, you will leave your mark on the next generation.

You can mentor people outside your family too. I hope by now this is already happening. Remember, you were designed for this (Titus 2:3–5; 2 Tim. 2:2). And by this phase of life, you should be well armed with both spiritual wisdom and countless life experiences that add wit and insight to your outlook for helping younger people better live their lives.

MARRIED, AND YOU'RE AN IN-LAW AND GRANDPARENT

Wise Moves

- Your role as grandparent is vital. Make the most of it!

- Continue your Kingdom work. "Invest down" in young people.

- Deepen your friendships and make new ones.

Key Verse:
1 Peter 3:8–11
2 Timothy 1:5

Late-in-Life Widow

"A single person is missing for you, and the whole world is empty."[2] These are the words Philippe Ariès used to describe the grief and displacement that follow the death of a loved one. It's an emptiness we are all destined to feel at some time or another, but among the living it is most often women who are robbed of the closest presence of all: that of a spouse. While only 7 percent of men age sixty-five and over are widowers, over a third of women in this age group are widows.[3]

Novelist Joan Didion is one such woman. As Ariès would say, Didion's world emptied shortly after Christmas 2003 when her husband, author John Gregory Dunne, died of heart seizure at the dinner table. Didion came home from the emergency room and tried to carry on as before.

The problem is, she kept trying to carry on *exactly* as before, as if John were due to arrive momentarily. She left his desk untouched. Open books remained so, ready for John's probing eye. His clothes and shoes were kept in place. He was coming home. It took Didion months to see the absurdity of her actions. She had forsaken the future for the past, something that's easy to do in this season of life.[4]

God cares for widows, and the Bible accordingly has a lot to say about them. Indeed, much of 1 Timothy 5 is specifically devoted to discussing the subject of older and younger widows. Younger widows, according to the apostle Paul's instruction, should seek to reenter married life (1 Tim. 5:14–15). Their mind-set needs to be more "single" than "widow." That means dating again; focusing on a career; and preparing for marriage again, possibly even kids. Paul's message is clear: God wants younger widows to reengage in mainstream life as much as possible rather than languish as untimely victims. My friend Sandy Bone, whose story I told in the opening of this chapter, is a prime example of how this can be done.

Older widows (those over sixty years old, according to Paul; 1 Tim. 5:9) will have a different rhythm. Life's opportunities have narrowed. It's not that remarriage is out of the question. It's not. And it's wonderful when it happens. But for many, remarriage is not realistic or necessary. There are many other good things to live for: grandchildren, friends, serving others, various kinds of Kingdom work, mentoring, and prayer, to name a few. If these things have already been a meaningful part of your life as a woman, then these cultivated habits of the heart are not hard to expand on. If not, now is the time to expand your life beyond yourself.

The real oxygen of life is in giving. Nowhere is that better seen than in the last seasons of life. Selfishness doesn't work here. Nothing is more pitiful than a demanding, self-absorbed, grasping old person. You've seen this. A stingy old person is far more disturbing than the most self-absorbed child could ever be. On the other hand, few things are more radiant and vibrant than a loving, other-centered, grace-filled senior. Jesus was right.

It is "more blessed to give than to receive" (Acts 20:35). And nowhere is that truth illustrated more clearly than in the way people look and act as life is wrapping up.

For more than twenty-five years I have watched young people fill the home of Kitty Longstreth, a longtime widow. I have met few people as alive as Kitty. Now eighty-five, she has

---

LATE-IN-LIFE WIDOW

Wise Moves

- Serve others.
- Mentor younger women.
- Do Kingdom work.

Key Verse:
1 Timothy 5:10

devoted her "alone years" to encouraging, praying for, and serving others. Many people in our community would say they owe their spiritual lives to Kitty. Almost any hour of the day, a young woman is at Kitty's house, where she is pointed to God. And as much as Kitty has blessed others, this posture of giving and loving has made her own life equally rich and meaningful.

So don't waste your life looking back as an older widow. Focus instead on the good you can yet do in life. Devote yourself to others. Love. Mentor. Befriend the friendless. Show the strength of a woman who believes God's promises and works to see their fulfillment in her life.

Glorified Saint

On this earth you made only the barest beginning to your life. You knew this. Your heart told you so. Your Bible said it too. You believed your greatest adventures and your best joys were being reserved for this last season of your life.

And now you're here!

It's bigger and better than you could have ever imagined. There are surprises everywhere. But before you plunge into them, there is a powerful meeting you must have with God— one on One—to sum up the life you lived on earth. This should not come as a surprise. You were told throughout your life this moment would arrive. God spoke of it in His Word: "For we must all appear before the judgment seat of Christ, so that each one of us may be recompensed for our deeds in the body, according to what he has done whether good or bad" (2 Cor. 5:10).

Everything will be clear in this moment of infallible evaluation. Everything you did in your earthly life—as God's feminine image bearer—will be taken into account by the God who never forgets. For your acts of courageous faith and obedience, you will receive a reward that will awe and humble you (1 Cor. 3:10–14).

For faithlessness and worldly compromise, your loss of reward will hurt (v. 15).

God will also give you new responsibilities and new treasures in heaven. Exactly what those are will be based on how well you followed Christ and God's Word while on earth (Matt. 19:27–30; 25:14–29). This is the clear teaching of Scripture (Matt. 6:20; Luke 12:33; 1 Tim. 6:18–19). For sure you are *in* heaven by the grace of God alone (Eph. 2:8–9). But it is equally true that your experience and standing in heaven will be shaped by the kind of life you lived while on earth.

So choose wisely before you reach this final season of life. Live a reward-winning lifestyle so that you can walk away from your coming appointment with God with His praise and commendation ringing in your ears (Matt. 25:21) as you step into a heavenly life of unimaginable rewards. No, you won't live a perfect life on earth. No one does that. You will know failure, compromise, and shame at times. But cling to faith. Repent from periodic bouts with unbelief and worldliness. And when you finish this life, finish as one who trusted God and was blessed by Him. Live this kind of life—the life of a New Eve—and you'll find that one of God's greatest delights is in giving you and others eternal rewards in heaven.

Every godly woman will find the same reality as she enters this final, glorious season of life.

Wisdom Is Now Vindicated

- Your wise moves on earth are rewarded by God in heaven.
- Your life is praised and commended by God.
- You are entrusted with new responsibilities and new adventures in God's eternal kingdom based on your earthly faithfulness to Him and His Word.

Key Verses:
2 Corinthians 5:10
Matthew 25:14–30

Faith pays off. Not only did faith reward her with the best of an earthly life (which she now fully understands), but it has now rewarded her with a rich heavenly life too. This promise is what every New Eve should hold on to and treasure in her heart.

Conclusion

So there you have it. Ten seasons of a woman's life. A wise woman will adopt this big-picture perspective as a general guide. From it she arms herself with the opportunity to make smart lifestyle choices that best fit and bless her changing seasons of life. Will that be you?

9

Choosing to Live with Purpose

These final words conclude the life of Abraham: "Abraham breathed his last and died, . . . an old man and satisfied with life" (Gen. 25:8).

What a way to go. This capstone statement reveals a life rewarded with a deep sense of personal fulfillment and gratification. It also suggests a life with few regrets. In short, life worked for Abraham. It came together with a wow rather than a whimper and paid rich dividends. Is there a woman or man alive today who wouldn't want a life like this? I don't think so. But the question is, What's the secret to living such a satisfied life?

Mary Crawford thought she knew. She was single, beautiful, and well versed in all the social graces. She dined with admirals, traded banter with barons, and flitted across ballroom floors under the watchful eyes of England's most eligible bachelors.

Edmund Bertram was one of those bachelors. He was widely known for his exceptional character and steady composure, but he couldn't disguise his interest in Mary. When Mary signaled for Edmund to make his case, he began plying her with questions.

When the discussion turned to the root of happiness, Mary said with stark frankness, "A large income is the best recipe for happiness I ever heard of." Edmund came from wealth, so Mary's reply played to his strong suit, right?

Wrong.

Though born into privilege and assured of a comfortable stipend for life, Edmund had little regard for riches. Mary was dismayed by this, but even so, she believed her future was with Edmund. Thus, she began a campaign to teach him better sense. Her future happiness depended on his discovering the importance of money.

Who is Mary Crawford? She is one of the central characters in Jane Austen's celebrated novel *Mansfield Park*. By the end of the tale, Mary's misplaced values are exposed in a drama that only Austen could compose. As a result, Mary loses noble Edmund as well as her dreams.

What happened? Her love of money and status—the very lenses through which she meant to bring happiness into focus— distorted her perception of reality. Convinced that money was the key to the good life, Mary participated in ploys and scandals that in the end undermined her credibility.

The Pursuit of the Good Life

Mary's outlook is relevant because it is shared by millions of Americans today. Money buys happiness, right? Actually, it often buys the opposite, especially when it becomes the goal of life. Even scientists say so. Dr. Edward Diener has studied money and its relation to happiness in great detail. He summarized his scientific findings in one short sentence: "Materialism is toxic for happiness."[1]

If love of money is toxic for happiness, what's the tonic? The answer: *purpose*. And it's a medically proven fact. Dr. William

Sheldon of Columbia University Medical School reported as much: "Continued observations in clinical practice lead almost inevitably to the conclusion that deeper and more fundamental than sexuality, deeper than the craving for social power, deeper even than the desire for possessions, there is a still more generalized and universal craving in the human makeup. It is the craving for knowledge of *right direction*—for orientation."[2]

In other words, we want to know how to do life right. Everyone hungers for a life that makes sense and is really going somewhere. But how do you get your hands on a life like this? Figuring that out is not so simple. Many people think it's life's best-kept secret. Novelist Peter De Vries once lamented that life was destined to remain a mystery: "If you want my final opinion on the mystery of life and all that, I can give it to you in a nutshell. The universe is like a safe to which there is a combination. But the combination is locked up in the safe."[3]

We would all be destined for sorrow if that were true. Without a satisfying purpose our spirits grow weak and listless. As Johann von Goethe put it, "A useless life is an early death." Fortunately, the converse is also true. People who've discovered purpose and meaning thrive in life. As Stephen Covey discloses in his book *The Seven Habits of Highly Effective People*, the happiest people among us are those who find life purposeful. They live life as a great big adventure that has a meaningful plot and a rip-roarin' conclusion. Or as Christians believe . . . a rip-roarin' conclusion that's just the beginning of an even greater adventure in heaven.

But living a purposeful life is not accidental. It doesn't merely happen. It requires a thoughtful process through which you carefully deliberate over various life options. Then, using certain preselected guidelines, you choose the options you believe have the best potential to deliver this life to you. For Christian women, studying and searching the Bible are huge assets in this undertaking because it contains a treasure chest of proven guidelines. Still, this process is intensely personal and soul-searching. You must also open *yourself*. Get personal. Go deep with intense questions and brutally honest self-examination. At some point you'll have to take a leap of faith and choose what and whom you intend to live for. These become the end goals of your life—your right direction. All of life is then lived in pursuit of them. They will shape and direct who you are. They will also become the primary measurements of your progress in life. Stephen Covey calls this "living with the end in mind." His research found that most successful people live this way. "To begin with the end in mind means to start with a clear understanding of your destination. It means to know where you're going so that you better understand where you are now and so that the steps you take are always in the right direction."[4]

Your Life's End

When I set out on a trip, what I believe about the destination dictates the choices I make and the actions I take throughout the journey. Am I driving to Florida with the kids? I believe it's sunny there and packed with beaches and theme parks. I pack shorts, shades, and short-sleeved shirts. I drive south rather than north. I gear up for pleasure rather than business. And if I remember the sunburn I got last time, I stop and buy sunscreen.

But what if it's the dead of winter and I'm heading to northern Michigan instead? It's cold rather than hot. I'm bound for business, not pleasure. I'd better not make the same choices I made for the Florida vacation. Where I drive and what I pack, as well as the plans and choices I make all along the journey, are all shaped by the destination.

Life is the same way. How you want your life to finish should be reflected in how you are living today. King Solomon understood this. This is why in Ecclesiastes 7:2 he said it's better to go to a funeral than a party. A party can lift your spirits, firm up your network, and introduce you to new friends and ideas. That's good stuff. But if it's meaning, happiness, and fulfillment in life you're after, you go to a funeral. You stand there and gaze uncomfortably at the deceased, not sure how long you should linger before moving on. You think of her life, theme, and legacy. What did she mean to you? To others? What mark did she make in life? Was it meaningful? Was it happy? Did it make a difference? Did it have any connection with eternity? You turn these questions over in your head and listen to the whispered comments all around you. Then you wonder what friends and family would say at *your* funeral.

That's what's so good about this moment. It brings the end to mind. *Your end.* It's natural here to ask yourself if you are measuring up. Do the choices you've been making count for anything? For what? You're on sacred ground now. You've penetrated the fog of daily existence and come face-to-face with what life is really all about: your end goals. So what do you see? Do you like what you see? If not, how as a woman, a wife, a mother, a worker, and a Christian would you like your life to end? Having done and become what? Giving your life to what? Leaving what to whom? Can you see it? Is it clear? Is it meaningful? Satisfying? Will it be meaningful in eternity?

It's healthy to ask yourself these sorts of questions. *Necessary,* even, if you want to be a New Eve. It's a step of bold, practical faith that will eventually lead you to a better life, as it has others.

The Now Lifestyle

Of course, there is an easier path. Many people—women and men—take it. It's a way of life that seeks the approval of the moment regardless of the long-term consequences. This lifestyle pays no heed to the insights of timeless wisdom. Today is all that matters. Cultural cues get all the attention. Whatever the world is saying, being *in* is of utmost importance. Forget the popular slogans and images of yesterday. *Now* is what counts.

A term paper written by a female Yale student exemplifies this way of life:

> Most Yale women ... aren't clamoring for equal rights
> or the chance to be called on in class anymore. They
> want a long wool coat for the winter, a Macintosh laptop
> computer with an MP3 player, a course load that doesn't
> include books by dead white men exclusively, a gay man
> for advice and a straight man for every other weekend
> or so, one good pair of Manolo Blahniks sometime
> in the future, to maintain a woman's right to choose,
> something to finally be done for the women being cir-
> cumcised in Africa and suffocated under burqas in the
> Middle East, a cigarette or a shot or a joint when the
> company is right, a husband at some point though no
> point soon, a good education, a GPA above 3.5, and a
> network of connections for when she graduates.[5]

This Now lifestyle is the opposite of living with the end in mind. Comparison and competition are its chief values. Do I look right? Do I look better than you? Do I have enough? Do I have more than you? Am I better positioned than you? Are my children outperforming yours? You chase after the latest and best with passion, never questioning whether it will be the right stuff in the end.

It rarely is.

My good friend Bob Buford is a gifted social observer. He especially loves analyzing what brings out the best in people. In his book *Finishing Well*, Bob relayed the following insight that he gleaned from Peter Drucker. Speaking of what he calls the "exemplars" or "heroes" of life—people whose lives have not only been successful but have actually gotten better over time—Drucker said, "They may not be smarter than the others, but the main difference between them and the nonheroes is that they *think ahead*."[6] Most people don't think ahead. They let life surprise them.

The Now lifestyle is a life primed for surprise but not the kind of surprise you're looking for.

Satisfying Legacy

Shakespeare wrote, "No legacy is so rich as honesty." I won't dispute the importance of honesty, but I would like to submit the following amendment: No legacy is so rich as a life lived with the end in mind.

The woman who lives this way has a rare perspective. Because she knows that one day she will face God, she orders her life to be God-pleasing and other-centered. She lives to make a difference she can identify now. With this end in mind she makes wise decisions and avoids foolish dead ends. She holds that course even when it is hard because she believes it will bring her great satisfaction. And like Abraham, she finds that her satisfaction with life grows with time. By life's end she has carved out a rich legacy of benefiting others through her works and passions. Her life and godly character have impacted her friends, her community, and her family. "Her children rise up and bless her; Her husband also, and he praises her, saying, 'Many daughters have done nobly, but you excel them all'" (Prov. 31:28–29).

How does this differ from the legacy so many women are forging as they adopt the world's ever-shifting values? Flip on *E!* or read *People* magazine, and you'll get a pretty good idea.

By definition a legacy is what you leave to others that echoes through the generations. Choices, habits, and circumstances can perpetuate themselves from mother to daughter and on down the line. Take rock star and quintessential bad girl Courtney Love, for example. Her mother, Linda Carroll, described her as "a whirlwind of rage and venom and passion in peroxide hair and lacy, torn dresses."[7] What led Courtney down this path? Her mother thinks it is in the genes. Courtney was born "with a biology that created internal torment," she says.

Was it really bad biology? When you read about Courtney and all the women who shaped her life, what comes into view is a legacy of living for now. Genes don't make choices, and choices are the things that have haunted Courtney and her foremothers. The story begins in the 1920s when a woman named Elsie gave birth to a baby girl named Paula Fox, who became the acclaimed author of dozens of popular books. But before Paula was a famous writer, she was a horribly neglected child raised by an "unfathomably cruel" mother. Elsie dropped Paula in and out of orphanages and veered in and out of her life like a destructive tornado. For Elsie, Paula was merely an obstacle, a distraction from the things she really wanted in life.

Naturally, Paula grew up confused about womanhood. She fooled around, made bad choices, and gave birth to baby Linda while in her teens. Paula quickly gave Linda away to a woman named Louella, who was in the middle of her own troubled storyline of rejection and bad behavior. For the next eighteen years Louella kept a safe distance between herself and her adopted little girl who longed for love. Indeed, Linda's entire childhood was marked by a hunger to belong to someone—*anyone*.

When Linda came of age, she looked for love in all the wrong places. There was casual sex, thoughtless marriage, and nonchalant divorce. There were bongs and binges, communes and cult leaders. Linda's firstborn child, Courtney, picked up on this legacy of poor choices alarmingly early. At age nine Courtney was caught with pornographic magazines. At age twelve she got drunk and cut herself up. By age sixteen she was on her own, earning a living at strip bars around the world. The rest is tabloid history.

So is all this merely the work of bad genes, as Courtney's mother claims? Quite the contrary. Courtney's life is simply the legacy of lost women with no noble, life-lifting purpose to their lives, making short-sighted, self-destructive choices. And those choices were not only destructive, they were also *instructive*. Courtney learned from the patterns set down before her and then personally pushed those patterns to new extremes.

This is why living with the end in mind is so important. It helps you not only live a fulfilling and productive life, but it also helps you leave a satisfying legacy. That's because the way you live your life is not only about you. Others are impacted!

Hard Choices

If you take God and His Word seriously as a Christian woman, you will inevitably face hard lifestyle decisions from time to time. That's because a rich and fulfilling life—one rewarded by God—requires moments of bold faith. *Bold faith.*

You will need that kind of faith for the hard choice between full devotion to a successful career or downshifting that career to raise a family. You'll also need it when choosing between Kingdom work or retiring; playing it safe or taking a new, gut-wrenching career risk; holding on to your children or letting them go; giving up on your marriage or courageously rebuilding it.

Hard choices and bold faith are part of the purpose-driven journey every New Eve is called to take. As you know, life can get messy. Sometimes doing the right thing causes life to become even harder. In times like these you must persevere because, despite the difficulties, you know that the path you are pursuing has eternal purpose and God's reward in it. You can draw encouragement that others have gone before you in this. Some of them faced choices and circumstances far harder than anything you're likely to encounter, and yet their end-in-mind perspective gave them remarkable courage and held them steady and true. Blandina, a slave girl who lived in Gaul more than eighteen hundred years ago, is one of the best examples I know.

We know next to nothing about her except that she was one of a handful of Christians in Lyons, Gaul (modern France), in AD 177. Christianity was still new there, but it had grown enough to become a nuisance to the locals and draw the attention of Roman Emperor Marcus Aurelius, who believed Christians were immoral and superstitious. Wishing to supply rich landlords with a cheaper means of gladiatorial entertainment, Aurelius fixed his gaze on the Christians. They were generally poor and uneducated, so he calculated that they could be rounded up and killed for sport at a tenth of what it cost to procure and dispose of professional gladiators. And so the band of local Christians was collected and forced into the bloodstained arena at Lyons, where they were presented with a stark choice: either blaspheme Jesus Christ or die. The frenzied crowd roared as first one, then another, and then perhaps a dozen others chose life over faith, but they roared even louder when dozens of the Christians chose death over apostasy.

For several days Blandina was brought to the arena but kept from harm. Her handlers believed that if she saw enough Christians needlessly die, she would renounce Christ and save herself. She watched soldiers strap a ninety-year-old man onto an iron chair that glowed red-hot. She watched animals maim and kill women as the crowd demanded more. Day after day she watched the horror, but she wouldn't give in. Eventually she was beaten and hung from a stake in the center of the arena. Miraculously, none of the beasts harmed her. Had an angel preserved her for a greater testimony?

Blandina was repeatedly beaten and slashed in the following days, and yet she stubbornly survived until the last day of the spectacle. By now she was famous. No one had ever seen such bravery in a woman. But how would she finish? Would she live with the end in mind even when one simple word, one bare moment of living for now, could save her life?

One last time Blandina was thrown into the arena. This time she was with the only other publicly known Christian left alive in Gaul—a fifteen-year-old boy named Ponticus. The boy kept the faith and died quickly, but his courage emboldened Blandina. She was bound in a net and then tossed before an enraged bull that hurled her around like a sack of straw. When the bull grew bored, the soldiers dumped Blandina's limp form from the net. She was still alive, and no, she did not wish to renounce Christ!

By now the judge had seen enough. He rose from his seat and shouted down his judgment: "Kill her immediately!" A soldier grimly obeyed. Blandina's remains were fed into a bonfire and then unceremoniously dumped into the Rhone River.[8]

Blandina's life was hers to save. All she had to do was renounce Christ and swear by the idols of Rome. Dozens of others had done exactly that. They forsook the end to live for the now. Blandina, a young girl with her whole life before her, could have joined them, but she made a better choice—a hard choice we're still talking about nearly two thousand years later. Why did Blandina give her life away? She gave it away because she knew God had given her life meaning and purpose, and she believed that in the end her courageous choice of faithfulness would be rewarded. It was this kind of bold faith that fueled the spread of Christianity throughout the Roman Empire and that ultimately came to you and me. One can only imagine Blandina's celebration at the judgment seat of Christ. Great is the reward for living with the end in mind!

Write It Down

I mentioned earlier that Stephen Covey said the happiest, most effective people have goals that purposefully direct the course of their lives. It's important to note that these aren't merely goals that float in and out of their heads when they have a spare moment to reflect. No, these are *written* goals that powerfully pull their lives forward.

You can benefit from the same practice. By recording on paper your end goals, you bind yourself to a contract with the future you. With God's help you commit to take every day whatever steps are necessary to get you where you want to be before your life is over. This is true end-in-mind living.

What's more, Covey found that people who write down their goals almost always end up overachieving. I've seen this principle at work in my own life. When I look back on the goals I set down on paper years ago—goals I hoped to achieve before my death—I find that I achieved most of them before age fifty. I would never have believed that was possible when I first wrote them in my twenties. Living with the end in mind helps to make good things happen—often sooner and better than you dreamed possible.

So, where do you want to be by the end of life? A New Eve will ask this question with utmost seriousness, knowing that her proactive engagement with these vital, ultimate issues will be one of the wisest moves she can ever make. Indeed, it is foundational to a happy and purpose-filled life. So pretend for a moment that tomorrow is your last day. Looking back, what do you see? What did you make of your life? What did you do? What did you become? What were you known for? What impact did you leave? It's in asking these kinds of questions that you give yourself—and the God who lives in you through His Holy Spirit—the opportunity to unlock the doors of purpose to your life.

Bobb Biehl can help you here. Bobb is a world-class business consultant and personal friend whose wisdom and insight have helped me through many tough spots. Each time we're together, Bobb offers me helpful exercises that enable me to keep my life focused and on track. I still carry one of those exercises (the chart on the next page) in my wallet.[9] I offer it here as a practical tool to help you begin consciously envisioning the end goals of your life and put them into print. Want to give it a shot?

Take a moment and see what comes to mind as you take a pencil and fill out the diagram on the next page. Don't try to fill out the whole diagram at this time. One or two simple answers under each column will suffice for now. For example, you might say I want to *be* a writer, I want to *help* orphans in my city, I want to *enjoy* traveling the world, I want to *have* healthy, well-adjusted children who know Jesus Christ, I want to *be* financially generous to others, especially in kingdom work. When you're finished, reflect for a moment on what you've recorded. Does it reflect what you *really* want in life? Does it reflect what you believe as a Christian? If it doesn't, what's missing? If it does, are the choices you are making right now moving you toward your goals? If not, why? As I said, this exercise is a simple way for you to begin formulating your life's end goals. So give it a try.

Before I die, I want to . . .

E	BE	DO	HAVE	HELP	ENJOY	LEAVE
N						
D						
G						
O						
A						
L						
S						

To make the most of this exercise, make a copy of this diagram and put it in your Bible. Periodically review and refine your end goals. Always use a pencil so you can make changes. In time, this should become your life compass.

Conclusion

The apostle Paul stated this advice best. To paraphrase him in Ephesians 5:15–17, be careful how you live your life, not as an unwise woman, but as one who is wise, making the most of your life, because the days are evil. Don't be foolish but understand the will of the Lord.

A New Eve takes this admonition very seriously. She doesn't want her life to be wasted. She wants it to be purposeful before God. She wants it to count. Therefore, she does whatever she can to make sure her life is pointed at those things that she knows count most. She works and prays to discern what the will of the Lord uniquely is for her and then lives in its light. This effort is the fourth bold move of every New Eve for navigating life successfully. Here it is:

Live with the end in mind.

10

Engaging a Man

They were on their way to a wedding.

It would be a lavish affair, so Carolyn had to have exactly the right dress. Something high-end, of course, but modest in appearance. Carolyn knew from experience that the photographers—there would be at least a dozen—would be as apt to shoot her as the bride, but the last thing she wanted to do was steal the show. After hours of searching the racks at Saks Fifth Avenue, she found what she wanted. As she left the store, Carolyn was surprised to see that the sun had already ducked well below the western edge of the cityscape. It was getting late. She'd better hurry.

Across town, John Kennedy Jr. noticed the time too. He picked up his sister-in-law, Lauren, and headed for the municipal airport as quickly as he could. But traffic was bad. So were the gawkers. Pedestrians, street vendors, and other drivers—they all craned their necks to get a look at John in his shiny white convertible. Traffic crawled.

By the time John and Lauren met Carolyn at the hangar, night was beginning to fall. John scrambled to get his small plane ready for takeoff. As a new pilot, he was not yet instrument-rated. He was licensed to pilot a plane only when visual conditions were good. He checked the darkening sky several times and listened to the FAA weather report.

All clear. John could handle this.

At twelve minutes after sundown, John roared down the runway in his Piper Saratoga. Carolyn and her sister chatted behind him. Moments after being airborne, a thick haze developed, veiling the sky. John struggled to see his way. He aimed his plane out over the ocean toward Martha's Vineyard. But as time went on, he began to doubt himself. He glanced down at his instrument panel, but it was no use. Too complex. The dials and numbers meant nothing to him.

As conditions worsened, John lost all his bearings. Up and down, water and sky—they looked the same. "You can be upside down and turning to the left and your body is telling you you're right side up and turning right," pilot Edward Francis later said of such conditions.[1] As Carolyn huddled with her sister, hoping for the best, John made a decision. Supposing that he was dangerously close to the water, he yanked the yoke toward his lap to gain altitude. His instruments told him not to do that—that his wings weren't level—but John didn't notice. Suddenly the Piper plunged seaward, caught in the grip of a violent corkscrew dive it never escaped.

Instrument-Rated Womanhood

John Kennedy Jr. lost his way and then his life because he had nothing to go on but his instincts. Unfortunately, those instincts failed him. And today instincts are failing many contemporary women who, like Kennedy, guess their way through life. Now more than ever, it's difficult for a woman to "read the skies." The view is clouded by new choices, new opportunities, and new conflicts.

In former times choice was the privilege of an elite few. Careers and social status for the less privileged were decided the day they were born. For the masses, life was narrowly defined. They did what was expected of them. For women, that almost certainly meant they learned the domestic trades as a girl and married before their twentieth birthday. That was the given of the times.

But the given of our era is that there are no givens. The playing field is wide open. Women can essentially do anything they want. As I've said, that's mostly a good thing. A freeing thing. But it also demands that today's woman be instrument-rated. She can't afford to fly blind in the twenty-first century when looking for satisfying womanhood. It's deadly when she does.

Instrument-rated womanhood means managing yourself by bold faith in God and His Word. It means refusing to trust your senses, especially when life gets dizzy and you're disoriented by worldly pressures and options. Instead, as a New Eve, you must trust your instrument panel. Respond to the dial that reminds you to always *live from the inside out* and stay with God's priorities even when a tempting opportunity tells you to abandon them. Another dial on your panel will steady you by helping you *keep a big-picture perspective* on life; another will point to *a biblical vision of womanhood;* still another, to *living with the end in mind.* Instrument-rated womanhood requires trusting the dials, not your instincts or the latest worldly visions.

Instrument-rated womanhood also means you must check the dials when engaging and choosing a man. Instinct alone in this area can be especially deadly. Love can be deceiving. You've seen the pain in the faces of close friends, business associates, and family members who've flown blind in this area. When it comes to men, a New Eve places her faith in something beyond intense and intoxicating emotions. She's much more savvy than that! Instead, she employs a fifth bold move to keep her steady with the men who come into her life. Here it is:

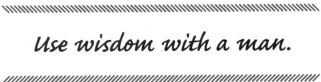

Use wisdom with a man.

This may sound simple, but it's not. It requires research and investigation. A New Eve studies the essential nature of men to understand and appreciate the inner workings and unchangeable characteristics of the male psyche. By doing so, she equips herself with a huge advantage that will go a long way toward helping her find happiness in a future relationship. To get you started in this direction, let's crack open the door on masculinity and examine what you must know and understand to successfully engage a man.

Four Fundamentals

What Drives a Man

Do you know what drives a man? Your man? Any man? Can you name the engine under the hood of his life that powers his get-up-and-go? I can.

It's called *performance*.

Performance is the force behind every aspect of a man's life. It's why men are consumed with winning, conquering, producing, and succeeding. Michelangelo spoke for all men when he said, "It is only well with me when I have a chisel in my hand." Men are life's ultimate action figures. As a woman, that's important for you to know. But what's even more important is for you to grasp that a man's whole sense of personhood and well-being centers on his performance. That cannot be stated strongly enough. George Gilder, a keen observer of social science, put it this way: "Manhood at the most basic level can be validated and expressed only in action. . . . Men must perform."[2]

When I was young, an oil company used to advertise its product with this slogan: "It's performance that counts." That, I believe, is the slogan of men everywhere. This performance mind-set drives everything men do. It's the reason men are reluctant to stop and ask for directions. To do so is to admit, "I haven't performed well. I've failed. I didn't cut it." A college biology teacher once asked his class the following question: "Why, in the reproductive process, does the female offer only one egg while the male offers millions upon millions of sperm?" A coed raised her hand and said, "Because those guys won't ask for directions either." She's probably right. It goes that deep! That's why men would rather drive on, hoping to get it right rather than pull over and ask for help.

In every area of life, men continually ask themselves, *Did I come through? Did I perform well?* That's a man's basic life question, and believe it or not, you as a woman play a crucial role in the way he answers that.

Yes, *you.*

In the classic fairy tale *Snow White and the Seven Dwarfs*, a wicked witch repeatedly asks her magic mirror this familiar question: "Mirror, mirror, on the wall, who's the fairest of them all?" Of course, she did not get the answer she wanted. The witch's torment was that the mirror regularly reminded her of her second-class status to Snow White. Eventually, that negative reflection drove her to murder.

Men have mirrors too. And these mirrors possess a tremendous power that can either affirm or undo them. Most men have two such mirrors; Christian men have three. As they stand before each of them, they pose a question similar to that of the witch: "Mirror, mirror, on the wall, am I doing any good at all?" In other words, "Am I doing the ultimate masculine activity—performing, delivering, coming through?" If his mirrors affirm him, a man feels good about himself. He powers up. But if these mirrors frown on him and reflect failure, disappointment, and shame, this loss will unleash in him the same frustration, anger, and humiliation the witch felt. Problem is, this is no fairy tale. This is real life, and what he sees in these mirrors has an impact on more lives than only his own.

So what are these three mirrors? For two-mirrored men, they are the woman in his life and his work. Christian men look into a third mirror as well: the Word of God. Each of these mirrors offers its own unique reflection of a man's daily performance. The workplace mirror reflects the value of a man's skills and his performance in using those skills. The Word of God mirrors something much deeper. It reflects to him the thoughts, secrets, and motivations of his heart (Heb. 4:12).

Then there's you.

You are a man's most personal mirror. In your eyes, face, and responses he receives an evaluation of his life in ways that are deeply important to him. In you, he sees and feels his life's worth most intensely. If you are wise, you will often reflect back to your man his best traits and accomplishments. And in tough times, when he's had failures, your reflection of belief in him will help him believe in himself again and not give up. The helper title Genesis gives you refers not only to what you do, but also to what you reflect. Positive reflections build up and empower a man. Conversely, show a man his failures daily, and he may eventually let his best self go for the dark side. To have his shortcomings rehearsed in your mirror on a consistent basis may cause him to lose his masculine will altogether. In the harsh glare of your criticism, it will whither. The truth is, your man will often become what you reflect back to him. Your mirror is *that* powerful.

Remember, performance is what drives a man. Therefore, never take your man's accomplishments or efforts for granted. Celebrate his victories. Even embellish them. In hard times major on the best in him. Encourage him in such moments by expressing your belief in him and his abilities. Fear of failure often holds a man back from trying. That's why your belief in him is so important. It helps him to believe in himself and go for it. In a man's world it's performance that counts. "Mirror, mirror, on the wall, am I any good at all?" What are you answering back to your man?

His Key Needs

In 1 Peter 3:7, the apostle gives husbands this command, "You husbands in the same way, live with your wives in an understanding way . . . since she is a woman." What wise advice that is! I tell men all the time that no man "speaks woman" naturally. It's an acquired language. It takes research, investigation, practice, and a big dose of humility to learn it.

But look again at 1 Peter 3:7, and you'll notice something there for you too. See it? It's found in the words *in the same way.* Though Peter is passionately exhorting men to acquire an understanding of women, "in the same way" reminds you that Peter has just said the same thing to women; that is, women need to work to understand men too, because men and women will always be alien beings to one another. It's the first principle of male-female relationships.

In this light you can never study the opposite sex enough. And a good place to begin your education is by mastering a man's key needs. This is absolutely fundamental to your success with a man. Do you know what those key needs are? Let me give you what I believe are a man's top four.

1. *Men need admiration and respect.* When I do premarital counseling with a couple, I ask them to read Ephesians 5, in which Paul spells out the marital responsibilities of husbands and wives. After they finish reading, I ask the young man to tell me what one word stood out to him in this text as his chief assignment in the marriage bond. Rarely does any man miss the obvious answer. "To love my wife," he says. Often after he answers, the bride-to-be smiles approvingly and grabs his hand. I then tell the young man, "Never stop telling your wife you love her. Those are the words she longs to hear—always."

Then I turn to the young woman and ask, "And, of course, your chief assignment is to love your husband, right?" Most often her reflex answer is, "Yes, of course." Then I ask her, "Where did Paul say that?" I usually sit quietly and let her poke back over Paul's words for a minute to find this command. But she won't find it because it's not there.

Why? Because the deepest need of a man in marriage is not to be loved by his wife but to be admired and respected. That's why Paul concluded Ephesians 5 with these words, "The wife must see to it that she respects her husband" (v. 33).

This is "Man 101" here, ladies. What love is to you, respect is to him. In your world "I love you" means everything. But on his planet the best thing he can hear is "I'm proud of you." Those words are the best "I love you" a man can get. And every time you praise your man in this way, you're speaking affirmation, strength, and satisfaction into the core of his masculinity, especially when you do it publicly. To say to him, "I'm so proud of you" in front of others . . . well, for a man, it just doesn't get much better than that. Nothing beats being admired.

2. A man needs your support in his work and dreams. Daniel Levinson's mammoth research work, *Seasons of a Man's Life*, revealed that the typical man marries a woman who he thinks will nourish his life vision and help him fulfill his life's work. Levinson also found that if a wife fails to do this or loses interest in what her husband does, the marriage relationship eventually becomes troubled. Why? Because men need their wives to stand with them in their work. They need their wives to identify with, appreciate, and value the work that defines their lives.

This support is particularly important in times of change, when a man thinks his best shot at success is to change jobs or career paths or take some risky shot at a better life. At such times the support of his wife is crucial. No, he doesn't need you to mindlessly submit to his daring ideas. That could wreck you both. On the other hand, he doesn't need you to dig in your heels out of instinctive resistance merely because it stirs up your insecurities. Rather than blind obedience or emotional stubbornness, what he needs is your wisdom, strength, and encouragement to think outside the box. Help him evaluate. He doesn't need you to always agree with him, but he does need you to always believe in him.

According to Levinson's research, a lot of men consider a risky career move in their late twenties or early thirties. That was certainly true for me. In my first job after seminary, I co-pastored a church in Tucson, Arizona. I had a wonderful time there serving a great group of people. During my stay the church experienced significant growth; we hired a number of new staff and built a wonderful facility. It was all coming together.

But then I got a call from old college friends back in Little Rock. They had recently started a new church and were renting space in a small private school. Actually, they were conducting their services in the school's unair-conditioned gym. My buddies asked me to consider moving to Little Rock to be their pastor. There were no guarantees. The pay was minimal. But my leadership opportunities would be significantly broadened to allow me to try some of the new and unconventional things I had dreamed of doing as a church leader.

I discussed this opportunity with Sherard, who at the time was pregnant with our second child and had just finished decorating our new home. I explained to her that the salary they were offering me would not be enough for us to buy a home in Little Rock. We would have to rent instead. I also told her that this new church had no facilities; it was meeting in a sweatbox—literally. "It's a huge risk to go," I said, "but this church has dreams like ours and offers greater opportunity for me to use my leadership gifts."

I will never forget what happened next. After a brief pause, she smiled and said, "Robert, you can do it. Let's go."

And we did. Together. Her support and encouragement gave me the boost I needed to take this flying leap that has now defined my life more than any other. As I write, I have had twenty-seven wonderful years at Fellowship Bible Church. Great things have happened. But it all started with a supportive wife.

There is one other area in which a man needs a woman's support. It's in the area of dreaming. Yes, dreaming. Men spend a tremendous amount of energy contemplating what else they could do with their lives. They constantly think, *Where is the best place for me?* A big asset to them is having a woman they can think out loud with about these things. You need to know this dream talk is often nothing more than merely that: talk. But it is still very important to a man. It helps him to process and coordinate his life, measure its value as well as its possibilities. The woman who lives with her husband in an understanding way knows this. She sees the value in being his sounding board. Some women, on the other hand, are confused and perplexed by a man's dreaming. It can scare them.

Listen to what one woman said in a newspaper article I read years ago:

> My husband is a nut. He'll sit around after supper and talk about how we should pick up and move to Alaska. If we both work, we'll have a real stake in the future in five or six years. We will spend all night talking about it and figuring out how we will manage. Will he go up there first and look for a job and a place to live? Or should we both go and hope for the best?
>
> A week later, he'll be sitting around talking about how he ought to be taking a couple of courses at the university towards his master's degree. It would make a big difference in his chances of getting ahead in his company.
>
> What do you do with a man like that?

Does your man bounce around like that when he dreams out loud? Even now I do that with Sherard. Men love to open their hearts to their women and dream about other possibilities ... that is, if it's safe. If a man's dreaming out loud is met with reactions like "That's crazy" or "You've got to be kidding," he'll shut down. Maybe forever. And that's a loss for both of you. So let your man dream with you. Support him with probing questions like "Why would you want to do that? Would that really be the best option for you?" Or you can affirm him by saying, "You could do that, and you would be good at it." Enter his dreams, and he'll love you for it.

A man is paying you a big compliment when he invites you to dream with him. He is saying, "I trust you with my heart."

3. A man needs a recreational companion. In his excellent book *His Needs, Her Needs,* Willard Harley comments that for a man, "spending recreational time with his wife is second only to sex."[3]

So what does that mean? It means that the couple that plays together *stays* together. Like the retiring medical doctor and his wife I mentioned in chapter 8 who bought Harleys together, a man feels a deeper level of intimacy and friendship with his wife when she engages him in his recreational passions. Now relax, ladies, I'm not suggesting you have to go paint-balling, cliff climbing, or stalk and shoot deer in the mountains to satisfy this need, but there are ways to connect. For starters you can educate yourself on his favorite sport. Watch it on TV. Take a class on it—they are out there. Or do what my wife did. When we first married, Sherard was about as quick to grab the sports page as I was the fashion section, which was *never.* But before long she realized how important sports were to me. The next thing I knew, she was beating me to the sports page. It was a smart move on her part. Best of all, my wife has become an avid, educated sports fan, and we're both loving every minute of it . . . together!

4. A man needs physical responsiveness. A while back someone handed me a copy of a woman's magazine that had conducted a survey listing men's and women's favorite leisure activities. It reported that the number-one leisure activity for men is sex. No surprise there. No man needs a magazine survey to tell him that. But I broke out in a cold sweat when I read that the number one leisure activity for women was *reading!* Sex was buried way down the list next to sewing. Go figure.

Men are physical creatures. Extremely physical, as you know. And depending on who you are as a woman—single or married—you must approach this male need very carefully.

If you are single, you must draw physical boundaries with your man. In this sexually promiscuous world, that is hard to do. It may even seem prudish. Early Christians probably felt the same way because immorality was everywhere in the Roman Empire. Contemporary Roman commentators described adultery as a common, everyday behavior. "Pure women," sang Ovid, "are only those who have not been asked."[4]

For a New Eve, the core callings of God, not the moral conditions of a particular culture at a particular time, are what shape her choices. That's why a single New Eve draws physical boundaries with a man.

I have had singles press me on how tight these boundaries should be. Some cite Paul's words in 1 Corinthians 7:1 in which he said, "It is good for a man not to touch a woman." Is that the boundary for Christian singles? Not even to touch one another?

I don't think so.

Paul's words were a response to some previous questions the Corinthians had written him, asking how they should conduct themselves in their sexually free city, where the temple of Aphrodite, the love goddess, towered two thousand feet above them from a nearby mountaintop. Given the context, it's clear that Paul's statement "not to touch" a woman is not a blanket prohibition against all forms of physical contact, including hugging, holding hands, and the like. Rather, he clearly had in mind a more serious touching. He is talking about sex. He used *touch* in 1 Corinthians 7 as a euphemism for *sex* much like the word *lie* is used for it elsewhere in the Bible. The NIV Bible rightly clarifies this in a footnote: "It is not good for a man to have sexual relations with a woman."

For a single woman who has a growing relationship with a man, certain kinds of physical contact can be appropriate. But any contact that tempts her or her man to yield to sexual relations is absolutely inappropriate. *Always.* That is where the boundary line must be drawn. And honestly, that boundary line can rarely go beyond occasional hugs, holding hands, and some light kissing. Beyond that lies trouble. And the wise single draws those lines long before any physical contact begins with a man.

For the married New Eve, sexual restraint is not the issue. Sexual fulfillment *is.* You must meet the sexual needs of your husband. Those needs are not just physical but emotional too. After addressing singles in 1 Corinthians 7, Paul then spoke to married women and said that a wife must fulfill her (sexual) duty to her husband (v. 3).

The word *duty* may sound a bit strong here, but Paul used it to make sure a wife embraces sexual fulfillment with her husband as that important. Willard Harley wrote, "When a man chooses a wife, he promises to remain faithful to her for life. He makes this commitment because he trusts her to be as sexually interested in him as he is in her. . . . Unfortunately in many marriages, the man finds putting his trust in this woman has turned into one of the biggest mistakes of his life. He has agreed to limit his sexual experience to a wife who is unwilling to meet that vital need."[5] Why is that? I believe it's because many wives have not seriously considered their husbands' sexual fulfillment as their duty. The Bible says it is.

What is it that sexually fulfills a husband the most? Are you ready for this? It's *your* satisfaction that satisfies him the most. When your husband knows he has performed in a way that succeeds with you and gives you pleasure, life could not be better. This is a huge emotional longing behind your husband's sexual drive.

Many wives would never guess this. They assume what a husband wants most is to please himself. Nothing could be further from the truth! I've asked thousands of husbands what gives them the greatest sexual pleasure in their marriages. Almost universally, they tell me their deepest fulfillment is not in what they get, but in how well they pleasure their wives. It's that performance-that-counts thing again.

So sexual fulfillment for a husband is directly related to his wife's enjoyment. A husband loves it when he knows his wife really enjoys his lovemaking by the way she responds to him and compliments him. When that happens, a man feels like a *man*. A real man. It's the wise wife who makes sure her husband has no doubt about his manhood when he leaves her bedside. This is the duty a New Eve freely embraces.

Admiration and respect, support for work and dreams, recreational companionship, and physical responsiveness—these are the four top male needs every woman should master if she is to live with a man in an understanding way.

Three Things besides Love

What are you looking for in a man? Every woman has her checklist. Some lists are detailed with a host of highly defined specifics; others are merely general outlines. Whatever your list looks like, here are three questions you must check off before making any serious commitment to a man.

1. What was his home life like growing up? That script is probably the script he'll bring with him into your marriage, so the more you know about his upbringing, the better. He'll refer to it unconsciously and automatically when he makes gut reactions or responds to pressure. So quiz him about his childhood. Was it good? Difficult? Troubled? What are his most dominant childhood memories? What about his relationships with his parents and siblings? Healthy or broken? Who impacted him the most? Mom? Dad? In what ways? Are there open sores with them that remain unhealed? What was his parents' marriage like? What did he learn from it?

You see, a man's past may be a source of great strength and blessing to your relationship. Good things early in life can go a long way toward ensuring the same later in life. Unfortunately, the opposite is also true. A troubled past may foretell future trouble. The family suitcase a man brings with him may unexpectedly explode in your relationship, leaving you sorting through all kinds of hurt, confusion, strange behaviors, and unfinished business. Or he may keep all the pain there sealed up tight, leaving him mysterious, moody, angry, or demanding.

Unfortunately, you can't make him unpack that suitcase. It has to be *his* initiative, *his* commitment. But before marriage you should do a lot of probing. And if he's not interested in going there, odds are you'll be in for a rocky relationship at some point later on. But don't make it later on *as in marriage.* Know your man's past before you commit to marry him.

2. Is he a Christian? Scripture clearly forbids a Christian woman from being unequally yoked (that is, married) to a non-Christian (2 Cor. 6:14). Those who ignore this directive and eat this forbidden fruit will eventually taste the curse of this spiritual compromise. I have had hundreds of married women say the same thing to me: "If only he were a Christian . . ." In their voices is a tone of painful longing.

In his book *The Clash of Civilizations,* Harvard professor Samuel Huntington predicted in 1996 that the major cause of global conflicts in the future would be religious differences. He based that conclusion on his observation that religion is the heart of every major culture. Religion, he said, is the immovable right-and-wrong viewpoint people passionately cling to and want others to embrace, even if force is sometimes required.

September 11 proved Huntington right. The greatest global tensions in our world occur when the religious belief systems of different cultures are forced to rub against one another. And what's true of cultures is true of people merged by marriage. When people of two different religions marry (even if the religion of one is secular or atheistic), trouble will soon arise along the lines where their conflicting religious views meet. It's inevitable. And just as radical Islam now seeks to terrorize the West for its beliefs, you can be sure that conflicting religious beliefs will terrorize your marriage. That's why the Bible warns you not to be unequally yoked.

3. What has his past performance been like? Why this question? Because past performance is your best eye into your man's future performance. We use this same principle when hiring staff at our church. Barring something drastic, the past usually repeats itself. What has been will be again. It's the eye to how you hire; it's also the eye to how you marry.

So if you're single and dating, look closely at your guy's past performance with you and with other women. Has he been moral or immoral? Has he cared for you, or have you taken care of him? Has he been wild and crazy or steady and predictable? What he has been, he will be again. Can't share his heart and feelings before marriage? Don't kid yourself. That won't change after marriage. Poor work habits before marriage? Same after you're married. Bad finances? Same again. You'll be wresting the checkbook from him and trying to manage the finances before your bank account bottoms out.

Now I'm not saying he *cannot* change. I'm only saying don't count on it. A wedding ring will not morph him into some newly minted white knight. And you won't change him either. Only he can change himself. His past is your best eye into the future.

Practice the 10 No-No's

1. Never commit to a man based on what he could be. Make sure he *is* what you want, or else you will spend the rest of your life trying to change him to what he should be, and you won't enjoy that any more than he will.

2. Never have sex with a man before marriage. Sex before marriage is not an advance for women's liberation; it's a man's liberation from responsibility and a woman's downfall. When you have sex with a man before marriage, you release him from his call to a greater commitment to you. You douse his noble, masculine instincts by inflaming his baser passions. If you could see half of what I've seen in counseling, you'd see that sexual liberation is open war against the life most women really want with a man.

3. Never submit to anything immoral or illegal with a man. Don't sign prenuptial agreements either. Marriage is an all-or-nothing deal. And at no point in marriage should you sign legal papers your husband puts in front of you that you don't fully understand. Get the facts before you sign.

4. Never stay silent about abuse. Seek outside help if there is physical or emotional violence in your marriage or dating relationship. If you're married, remember that marriage is a community project, not a contract of silence. It might be hard to open up to others because you're afraid of what you might lose. But if you've got an abusive relationship, what you're holding on to will never get better in secret. Start by opening up to a trusted friend, family member, pastor, or counselor. Let this person give you perspective and then coach you on what to do next. If you are feeling abused, do this now!

5. Never nag. There are better ways to address problems in your relationship such as a direct, face-to-face dialogue about what is bothering you. If that fails, seek outside help. But don't nag. Nagging is jeerleading, not cheerleading, and it never improves a man. It only hurts him. As I mentioned earlier, one of the worst things a man can experience is looking daily into the "mirror" he loves and seeing his faults and shortcomings relentlessly being played back to him.

In my pastoral experience I've found that many unhappy marriages are actually pretty good overall. The problem is, husbands and wives tend to get locked in on each other's negatives. They lose sight of all the positive things about their significant other. As someone once told me, "You can blot out the sun with your thumb if you bring it close enough to your eye." You can also blot out a good marriage if you focus only on the things your husband is not. For this reason Scripture encourages women not to nag (Prov. 21:9, 19).

6. Never embarrass your man in public. Proverbs 12:4 says, "An excellent wife is the crown of her husband, but she who shames him is like rottenness in his bones." Nothing can anger a man more than being criticized by his wife or girlfriend in front of his peers. Even something as simple as rolling your eyes to mock his words or behavior before others can devastate him. The reason? It shouts, "This guy doesn't have it together." He may not react visibly to this sort of thing in the moment, but inside he begins to harbor secret anger against you for this public shaming. And that anger will often come out later in a different time and context.

7. Never stop cheering for your man, even when he has flaws. There's no perfect man or perfect marriage. Don't fall into the trap of idealizing other couples and their outwardly perfect marriages. Still, many women embrace marriage perfection in their minds. This mirage unnecessarily undercuts and stokes dissatisfaction in their own marriages.

I've seen many women struggle to accurately gauge the health of their marriage. Most are more pessimistic than they should be, dwelling on the 5 percent that's out of whack, to the exclusion of the 95 percent that's on track. Everyone else thinks, *What a great guy her husband is!* because he's doing so many things well. He's responsible, kind, truthful, and helpful, but she's lost sight of her great guy because she's locked in on the small percentage of things he's not doing well: "He doesn't talk to me enough. He's not a strong, spiritual leader in our home." Resist this negative approach. Don't dwell on a few shortcomings. Cheer the good stuff and entrust the rest to God.

8. Never treat sex in marriage casually. It's crucial to your husband. Crucial! Remember, good sex for a man is not only what it means for him but also what it means for you. Stay creative. Surprise him from time to time. Books are available to help you in this. Stay attractive. Tell him what he's doing right and how good he makes you feel. Good sex is life-giving to a husband.

9. Never assume his job is not your business. A man wants to marry a woman who will nourish his life vision. You should have a good hands-on knowledge of what your husband does and appreciate the pressures he faces. Interact with him when he needs to talk about his work. Problem solve with him when you can. Pray for him and let him know it. Be his career partner.

10. Never fall more in love with your kids than with your husband. That's easy to do as the years go by. I call it "the great swap." You get caught up in all the things the kids are doing, often seeing more of them than you do your husband. What you don't notice is the growing distance developing between you and the man you vowed years ago to give your life to.

Then comes the day when the house is empty of children. They're gone. But so is the closeness between you and your husband. You're alone with a stranger. Don't let that happen. Keep developing new ways to enjoy each other even while the kids are home. Take regular getaways without the children throughout your marriage to renew and refresh your relationship. Keep finding new ways to connect and enjoy life together. And when that day comes when the last kid moves out, you'll be able to turn to your husband and say, "At last! Let the good times roll!"

Conclusion

Much of the happiness a woman will achieve in this life will be in direct proportion to how well she engages the man in her life. As I pointed out in the beginning of the chapter, flying by sight with a man isn't going to be good enough to get you where you want to go. Every woman needs something more to be successful with a man. The New Eve knows this something more is wisdom. Sound wisdom. Biblical wisdom. It's this instrument, not her instincts, that guides and empowers her relationship with her man.

11

*The Best Marriages—
The Happiest Wives*

Sherard and I were married three days after Christmas in 1971. Ever since, remembering Jesus' coming to earth and at the same time marking our wedding anniversary make for an extended time of celebration with family and friends. We like it that way. There's love in every direction.

This past Christmas Sherard and I marked thirty-five years of marriage. Perhaps in light of this special milestone, I became a bit more reflective. I vividly remember our wedding ceremony and that moment when we raced to my car through a hail of rice to drive away as husband and wife and begin our new life together. I also remember thinking that day how thankful I was that I had a game plan for my marriage.

My parents lacked that in their marriage and for this reason they really struggled at times. What I saw in their relationship was not something I wanted repeated in mine. The opportunity for something different began when I was introduced to Jesus as a freshman in college. A few years later, while seriously pursuing Sherard, Christian friends invited us to study marriage from

165

a biblical perspective. Looking back, I'm glad to say that much of what I received then was accurate, balanced, and extremely practical. One statement I held on to during that instruction was my teacher's comments about Jesus' words in John 10:10: "I came that they may have life, and have it abundantly." After reading this verse, my teacher made the following remark: "Jesus' main reason for coming to earth was to give you a life better than any you can create for yourself. And that applies to your marriage too."

A better marriage is certainly what I wanted. Sherard too. So in the months leading up to our wedding day, we committed ourselves in faith to the biblical blueprints for a Christian marriage.

Marriage by the Book

What is God's design for marriage? And is it really better than the alternatives? Let's address the first question by looking into the Scriptures, and the second by looking at modern social research.

The biblical outline for marriage is relatively simple. We could sum it up this way:

- God the Father is the Lord of marriage, charging the husband and the wife with specific callings for their marriage (Gen. 1:28; 2:24).
- The husband is charged by God to be the head of his wife (Eph. 5:23).
- The wife is charged by God to be the helper of her husband (Gen. 2:18).
- The husband is to love his wife in ways that meet her deepest needs: giving her security, making her feel highly valued and significant, giving her conversational companionship, and being emotionally responsive to her (1 Pet. 3:7).
- The wife is to love her husband in ways that meet his

deepest needs: giving him admiration and respect, providing him personal support, joining him as his recreational companion, and being physically responsive to him (Eph. 5:33).

- Children are to be valued as gifts from God requiring time, sacrifice, personal attention, and training (Ps. 127:3; Prov. 22:6; Deut. 6:6–7).
- Children are to be raised to embrace a vision of changing the world and advancing God's kingdom with their unique gifts (Ps. 127:4–5; 1 Pet. 4:10; Gen. 1:28).
- The Holy Spirit is the conscience and the power that makes this kind of marriage possible (John 14:25–26; 16:8–15).

This is the biblical outline. Today, however, parts of it have become controversial among some Christians, especially the marriage roles of helper and head. Many modern marriages no longer embrace these biblical terms and therefore refuse to use them in their wedding ceremonies. In these cases Scripture is used highly selectively, omitting anything that might appear sexist. Most couples today are launched into their marriages on vague generalities of love rather than with specific biblical responsibilities. The only clear mandate is that the husband and the wife must be viewed as the *same*.

The biblical marriage, however, is a radically different construct. It's true that Scripture recognizes first and foremost that men and women are created as spiritual equals before God. Both equally share God's divine imprint and image (Gen. 1:27). As a couple, both husband and wife are to live together as coheirs, sharing equal honor (1 Pet. 3:7). But as male and female, they also have their differences. In marriage their functional roles are gender-specific.

Head

The Bible declares the husband to be the head of a marriage. This is not a title conferred on the man as a result of sin and the fall, as some have suggested. This is part of God's original design for marriage from the beginning.

In Genesis 2 (pre-fall), God created the man first. From a biblical standpoint this is not accidental but highly instructive. *First* implies *leader*. Thus, by creating the man first, God sent a clear message about social positioning between a man and a woman in a marriage relationship. Had God wanted the marital roles to be the same, He would have made the man and the woman at the same time. But He didn't . . . by design.

It's the same social statement I make at the end of weddings I perform when I pronounce the couple husband and wife. After doing so, I have them turn and face the audience. At which point I present them as "Mr. and Mrs. _____," always using the *husband's* name. Why the husband's name? The reason goes all the way back to the beginning of time, when God made the same statement by creating Adam first. In both of these symbolic acts, the man is recognized as heading this new relationship. Today, however, you have no doubt noticed more and more couples choosing to be recognized by their names being hyphenated together. This too makes a strong social statement. It says that no one heads this marriage.

Back in Genesis, Adam's headship was also seen in the tragic events of chapter 3 when both he and Eve plunged the world into spiritual darkness. But notice it was Adam, not Eve, whom God called to account for this rebellion. He was the one God held responsible for it. Indeed, the whole debacle was laid at Adam's feet. The New Testament states it this way: "Through one man sin entered into the world" (Rom. 5:12). This statement makes sense only if God gave Adam a unique leadership role with his wife, a role the New Testament openly recognizes when it calls a husband the "head of the wife" (Eph. 5:23).

When a man fulfills this role correctly, no one is happier than his wife. In more than thirty years of pastoral ministry, I have never once had a wife issue a complaint against a husband who leads in the way the Bible describes. Cheer, yes. Complain, no. On the other hand, the husband who uses the title of headship as a cover for control, dominance, or even abuse is not only *not* a head in the way the Bible sets forth but is instead a moral and spiritual failure. Let me make this clear: When it comes to a man's leadership in his home, male domination is never a teaching of the Bible. But headship is. It has been a married man's role since the beginning of time. And it requires from a man that he love, lead, protect, and provide for his wife and family with a servant's heart. Simply put, he is to lead as Jesus leads His church (Eph. 5:23). Headship is a demanding title that challenges every Christian husband to measure the day-to-day reality of his leadership by looking up to the ultimate Head.

Helper

Genesis 2 unveils the wife's role as helper. In verse 18 we read, "The LORD God said, 'It is not good for the man to be alone; I will make him a helper suitable for him.'"

Few situations can better illustrate the meaning of what God had in mind here than when a young bachelor marries. Go to his apartment or house before the wedding, and more than likely you will find a tasteless, colorless, Spartan environment. Just the basics ... and a few electronic toys. A weight set, TV trays, and mismatched sofas circled around a fifty-inch plasma screen compose the living area. There is nothing green or alive anywhere. The bedroom is dormlike; the bathroom, radioactive; the kitchen, unused except for a well-worn microwave oven. This is man *alone.*

But then he marries. In the weeks and months that follow, a miraculous transformation occurs. His house becomes a home. What was previously formless and void begins to spring to life. Order, form, color, art, warmth, heart, love, and laughter fill what was once nothing more than a utilitarian staging area. More often than not, the man quickly falls in love with these startling makeovers. He had no idea until now that he needed this much help!

The title of helper actually puts a wife in very elite company. After all, the Hebrew word for *helper* is used for God Himself. By the time you get to the end of the Bible, each member of the Godhead has been presented as a Helper to man. In Psalm 54:4, David said of God the Father, "God is my Helper; the Lord is the sustainer of my soul." This is a magnificent picture of the Creator of the universe lending aid to His frail creatures, but it also indicates the honor and dignity of being a helper. Jesus, too, became our Helper. Romans 5:6 gives a powerful picture of this truth: "While we were still helpless, at the right time Christ died for the ungodly." Jesus helped us when all other help failed. Finally, Jesus called God the Holy Spirit our Helper. In John 14:16–17, He said, "I will ask the Father, and He will give you another Helper [that is, One like Jesus], that He may be with you forever; that is the Spirit of truth." Who can doubt a wife's place of honor and worth when she bears the same title as God Himself?

All this is good news for husbands, for if anything is clear in life, it's that a man needs help. And the kind he needs most to succeed in life is one that is distinctly feminine. It is a help that receives, admires, nurtures, responds, supports, and loves.

A man grows by this kind of help. He matures. He is strengthened to reach higher and do more than he ever could without it. The truth is, every man *longs* for this kind of help.

These are the gender-specific roles God designed for every man and woman in marriage. Head and helper energize each other. They fit the social, spiritual, and relational dance God has in mind to call out the best in a couple. Rightly lived out, these roles unleash power, life, and intimacy into a couple that supersede any other symbiotic relationship on earth.

What is a biblical marriage? Using these titles of helper and head, along with the core callings for marriage we learned about in chapter 4, plus specific statements on marriage from the New Testament, we can answer that question with the following diagram:

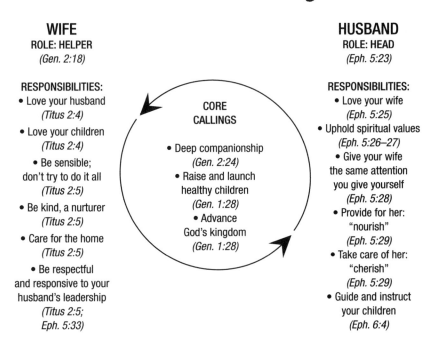

The Biblical Marriage

WIFE
ROLE: HELPER
(Gen. 2:18)

RESPONSIBILITIES:
• Love your husband
(Titus 2:4)
• Love your children
(Titus 2:4)
• Be sensible;
don't try to do it all
(Titus 2:5)
• Be kind, a nurturer
(Titus 2:5)
• Care for the home
(Titus 2:5)
• Be respectful
and responsive to your
husband's leadership
*(Titus 2:5;
Eph. 5:33)*

CORE CALLINGS
• Deep companionship
(Gen. 2:24)
• Raise and launch
healthy children
(Gen. 1:28)
• Advance
God's kingdom
(Gen. 1:28)

HUSBAND
ROLE: HEAD
(Eph. 5:23)

RESPONSIBILITIES:
• Love your wife
(Eph. 5:25)
• Uphold spiritual values
(Eph. 5:26–27)
• Give your wife
the same attention
you give yourself
(Eph. 5:28)
• Provide for her:
"nourish"
(Eph. 5:29)
• Take care of her:
"cherish"
(Eph. 5:29)
• Guide and instruct
your children
(Eph. 6:4)

What the Research Says

It's one thing for the Bible to set forth what it touts as God's design for marriage. It's another thing to ask, But is this really the best marriage arrangement? Is it the best for women? As any Eve knows, there's a host of other alternatives out there to pick from.

Sociologists Steven Nock and Brad Wilcox of the University of Virginia think they have some answers about which sorts of marriage models work best for women. Based on the findings of the National Survey of Families and Households, their research provides hard data on which type of marriage makes most women happiest.[1] Let me summarize six of their conclusions that Wilcox gave in an interview with *Christianity Today.*

1. Wives are happiest when they experience their *husband's emotional engagement.* This means a husband is affectionate, sympathetic, and "tuned in" to his wife's key needs. Emotional engagement is by far and away the single most important factor in a woman's happiness in marriage.

2. Wives who are in *neo-traditional marriages* (where the husband has the lead for breadwinning and the wife has the lead for nurturing) are happier and more stable than wives in other less traditional marriages.

3. Wives who along with their husbands *attend church on a weekly basis* are happier in their marriages than other women. The idea that Christians are just as likely to divorce as non-Christians is not correct *if* regular church attendance is factored in. If so, such marriages are not only happier, but they are 35–50 percent less likely to end in divorce. Husbands who attend church regularly are also more likely to spend quality time with their wives

and more likely to express affection to them than husbands who are not regular churchgoers.

4. Wives whose *husbands earn the lion's share of the marriage income* (at least 66 percent or more) are happier than other married women. They are also more likely to spend quality time with their husbands. When a husband is a good breadwinner, his wife is afforded more freedom and more life options, which contribute to her happiness.

5. Wives who have more *traditional gender attitudes* are significantly happier in their marriages than other women. They're also more likely to embrace the idea that men should take the primary lead in breadwinning and women should take the primary lead in nurturing the children, managing the home, and managing family life.

6. Wives whose *husbands do a fair share of the housework* are happier than other married women. It is extremely important that a wife considers the division of the housework to be fair to her. A sense of equity is important, but equity is *not* equality. Happy wives want things to be fair, but they don't equate fairness with equality.[2]

If you think all the points above seem to closely resemble the biblical marriage I outlined earlier, you're right. Whether they know it or not, Nock and Wilcox have generally described the marital blueprints God set down in His Word. These always have and always will produce the best marriages and the happiest wives.

Conclusion

What the Bible outlines as God's design for marriage has been a life-giving asset for Sherard and me. Despite a number of hard times, it has kept our marriage relationship strong, energized, and deeply unified.

This past Christmas all four of our children were able to be home with us, including Elizabeth's husband, Brent, and their son, Drew. For a few moments before opening presents, we each reflected back on the good things God had done in our lives for which we were grateful. It turned into a holy moment. Soon there were tears of joy flowing in all directions for the better things God had blessed our family with: answered prayers, significant life change, new freedom from bad habits, deeper relationships, a healthy baby, new understanding about life and God, and surprising, undeserved opportunities. As I listened, my heart was filled with praise and gratitude. It was all because of God and the plan, partnership, and power He graciously brought into my marriage thirty-five years ago when Sherard and I reached out and believed.

12

Your Biggest Challenge, Your First Bold Move

The early evening air was crisp and scented with autumn leaves as Susan arrived at the church. Children ran and laughed on the playground, playfully evading their parents who tried to collect them in the fading light. Susan stopped to watch. She thought of her childhood in Boston and her enchanted visits with Grandma in rural Massachusetts—the laughter, the ease, and the togetherness the whole family enjoyed over meals and backyard games. But that was before her parents divorced. Before she learned about relying on no one.

Now twenty-six, Susan was a world away from the family life she'd once known. Her house was in Raleigh, North Carolina, but she was a citizen of the world. As a hard-charging MBA, Susan aimed for the top. To prove her hunger, she traveled anywhere the company asked. Trouble in Chicago? Send Susan. There was nothing she couldn't do in a seventy-hour workweek. The Seattle staff needed training? Susan was the one. Boston, Los Angeles, San Antonio, anywhere, anytime. Susan's was a life in transit, and the transit began every Monday at 4:00 a.m. when she woke up, hopped a plane, and didn't return home until Friday night.

The money was good, but other priorities suffered. Saturdays were for crashing, and Sundays for church and maybe a quick visit with a friend. By Sunday afternoon she was packing for another workweek somewhere. Where did dating fit in? It didn't. But what choice did she have? Her career goals were as yet unrealized. She couldn't slow down now.

As she watched the last child hop into a waiting van, she sighed and turned to walk on to her Sunday evening meeting. She looked down at the book she was carrying.

Me, a New Eve? she thought. *I just don't know.*

◆

On the other side of the playground, Patricia had just finished parking her car. She'd seen Susan walking along the sidewalk across the way and watched her pause to look at the children. *What's she thinking about?* Patricia wondered. *She's young, talented. What does she want from life?* Patricia felt she had a pretty good idea. She had Susan pegged for a single-minded careerist. *So how has she been processing this New Eve study we're in together?* Patricia wasn't yet sure. Since their meeting was set to start in five minutes, Patricia gathered her stuff and hurried into the church. But she did so with anxiety.

As a fifty-one-year-old business executive who had never married, Patricia had learned to be guarded around other Christians. They meant her no harm, of course, but Patricia often felt edged out of church life. People didn't know what to do with her. She didn't fit their categories or expectations. She didn't have kids or grandkids to chat about or a husband whose foibles she could laughingly reveal to a circle of sympathetic women. But the differences didn't end there. She had traveled the world on business and now was earning more money annually than most couples earn in years. All of this pushed Patricia to the outside. The truth is, she often felt more alone in church than anywhere else in her life.

How can I be a model Christian woman when I don't fit the expected mold?

◆

Susan and Patricia met in front of the church and began to enter when they heard a car pull up in the lot behind them. They turned to watch Tracey zip her minivan into position next to Patricia's Mercedes. Tracey was a thirty-year-old, stay-at-home mom with two young kids and a baby on the way. She was barely holding it together.

"I made it!" she exclaimed with a big smile as she got out. "I told Trevor I can't be late again, so he got the kids distracted for me, and I rushed out of the house before they noticed! Isn't it crazy what a woman has to do to get out of the house?"

Patricia and Susan exchanged a humored glance. Neither of them could relate to Tracey's experience, but they enjoyed her open and fun-loving spirit.

When the three of them reached the meeting room, they found Anne scurrying around putting the finishing touches on a veritable buffet table of fruits, dips, and sweets.

"Anne, what on earth have you done?" asked Patricia in amazement.

"Oh! Just some finger foods. It wasn't any trouble at all."

"Looks like a *lot* of trouble to me," said Tracey. "Thanks so much for doing this!"

They mingled and munched for a while, and then Patricia suggested they start the meeting.

"But what about Brenda?" Tracey asked. "I'd hate to start without her."

Susan agreed. "Brenda's been stressed out lately. She and John are struggling. They're barely communicating right now. That's a hard way to start a second marriage."

"That's for sure," replied Anne. As an empty nester, Anne was happily married. Her children were reasonably healthy and well adjusted. To this point, life had been fairly smooth, but Anne found herself regularly asking, "What now?" It disturbed her that she had no ready answer.

◆

Brenda came in a few minutes later, looking embarrassed.

"Hi, everyone! Sorry I'm late."

"That's OK," the group said in unison. Brenda set her purse down and went for a quick stop at the refreshments table. "This is just what I needed," she said. "I've been running nonstop all day. Thanks for taking the time to do this!"

"Thank Anne," Susan quickly interjected. "She came early and did everything."

"How sweet of you, Anne!" said Brenda. "Thanks so much."

"Well, you're very welcome. I'm happy to help."

Brenda settled down into a seat and insisted that they not delay any further on her account. Anne, who had accepted the challenge to be the discussion leader, took charge.

"Well, we've all read and discussed the book," she said. "Tonight we agreed to write on an index card our biggest challenge to being a New Eve. So let's take turns sharing what we wrote. Who wants to go first?"

Susan decided to open the discussion. Besides, she had to be on a plane in less than twelve hours. No time for procrastination. She grabbed the card from where she had lodged it in the book and held it up for all the ladies to read.

> ### *In career I trust.*

"There it is," she said. "No surprise, is it? My challenge is that I'm tempted to place my sense of personal value and security in my career. I'm single, twenty-six, and my career is going great. But I do struggle with having a more balanced personal and spiritual life. At least, reading this book makes me think that. But the thing is, I'm also struggling with the emphasis the book places on marriage, kids, and those things. I mean, don't get me wrong. I believe in the biblical principles, at least as an ideal. I do want to marry someday and have kids, but I just don't see why I should back off from my career and look for a man to come in and take care of me. I mean, my mom tried that, and look where it landed her. Dad left her when I was nine, and for the next ten years she waited tables at a greasy diner so my sister and I could eat and have clothes. I don't know. Sometimes I feel that the Bible and books like this one teach a paradigm that modern women can't follow. Honestly, can a twenty-first-century woman follow first-century advice? We're in totally different worlds."

Susan paused for a moment. Then she continued. "But then the flip side is, I look at my life now and ask, Do I really want to live like this forever? I'm scrambling up the corporate ladder, but is it worth it? I drive a nice car, but I only drive it to and from the airport. I have a huge professional network, but I'm lonely. My clothes come from the designer rack, but they can't cover all my needs. So what should my priorities be? Does God want me to ditch my career and go on a manhunt? Can I keep my career *and* have a family? It's confusing."

The ladies reflected in silence for a moment. Susan's openness about her struggles caused everyone to relax a little more. No one would be playing Ms. Righteousness here.

"I think I understand pretty well what you're going through," said Patricia. "On one hand, you feel that you'll be a dropout or just plain reckless if you alter your career for marriage and kids, but on the other hand, you don't want to be so devoted to work and so distrustful of married life that you end up fifty-something and alone, like me."

Susan started to backtrack. She had not meant to be insensitive to Patricia's situation, but Patricia politely waved her off.

"No, really. It's fine. Let me clarify what I mean. I'll begin by showing my card."

> *Did I miss the good life?*

"That's my fear," Patricia said. "I'm fifty-one. I never married or had kids. What I *have* had is a great career full of perks and advancements. Sounds like the dream life of some hard-shelled feminist, right? Only in my case, it's not. The truth is, I never set out to walk this kind of path. Not intentionally, anyway. When I graduated from college in the mid '70s, all I ever heard from the women I admired was that it was up to me to make my own way. Don't get stuck waiting for a man to take care of you. Show the world what a woman can do in the workplace. All of that made sense to me. A lot of it *still* does. But what happened is, I lost perspective. So did my friends and mentors.

"After college I took a series of tough jobs. Workplace equity was far from a reality in the '70s and '80s, so I worked harder than anyone else. After a while I got promoted. Then women everywhere were getting opportunities like never before. I was exhilarated to be part of the revolution. By the '90s I made VP in my company and was one of the best in my field. But then I realized I was breaking into my forties and was still single. Twenty years had blazed by since college, and all I had to show for it was a place at the boardroom table.

"Now that seat at the table was pretty good, but it dawned on me that I had shut down other important avenues for my life. For years I had lived project to project, challenge to challenge. I never made time for finding a mate. So then I took a stab at carving out more time for my social life, but there was always a desk full of work or another plane to catch. Besides, if I'm honest, I liked it that way. Work was what I knew. I was good at it. So I kept doing what I had always done. Now here I am. Another ten years have gone by. My career is awesome, but I'm still alone, and now more than ever, being alone actually feels lonely."

Anne reached over and squeezed Patricia's hand.

"Thanks," Patricia said. "It's hard sometimes, but I'm OK. I guess the thing I want to say, Susan, is that now is a good time for you to take stock of your options. You can do anything you want. You've got a great career going, and no doubt you can turn it into something huge someday. But you can also do something else. You can balance that opportunity by seeking other options I failed to consider—options that can save you from regret later in life. You might start by exploring the possibility of how to cut back on your work hours and . . . excuse me . . . your *insane* travel schedule.

Your company clearly values you. Tell them you're excited about your continued commitment to them, but that you want to travel less, be home more, and have a more normal life. Maybe there is another position at the company that better fits you and what you want in life. Certainly there's no harm in looking.

"Just know this: the steps you take now will go a long way in determining what your life will be like long-range. My advice is, decide now what you really want in life and then do what's necessary to get there. Don't put this off! It's too important. You might be surprised by what doors God opens up for you. I mean, He is with you in this."

"All that makes way too much sense to me," Susan said with a sarcastic laugh. "I certainly don't want to lessen my chances to have a family, but I just don't know if I can scale back the one part of my life that's working so well so that I can have a better shot at finding a mate. It could hurt my career, and there aren't any guarantees that I could be happily married anyway. So I guess what I'm saying is, Is a happy marriage anything more than luck? I don't feel secure when I think of entrusting my future to a marriage."

Brenda nodded her head vigorously. "My first marriage was certainly a reality check. Come to think of it, my second one isn't much better." She smiled, but everyone could feel the pain in her voice.

"Brenda, you know we're all praying for you," Patricia said as everyone nodded.

Anne then looked back at Susan. "All marriages have their hard moments," she said, "but I don't think the good ones are because of luck. I know for me it has taken work, compromise, tons of honest communication, and at times some huge leaps of faith. But Art and I have experienced a good marriage for almost thirty-two years. Looking back, I see the key has been the spiritual convictions we've both held on to. That and giving God all the hurts, confusions, and disillusionments that crop up from time to time. Oh, well, that's us. Maybe *your* biggest challenge for being a New Eve is a huge faith leap of your own. Maybe it involves letting go of the pain from your parents' divorce and trusting God for your life."

Susan's eyes dropped to the floor. "I think you're right," she said. "At base it is a trust issue. Do I trust God with my future? Right now I'm just not sure I can honestly say I do. Mostly I trust myself."

"So there's your bold move," Patricia said excitedly. "You've identified your primary obstacle to being a New Eve. Now the question is, Can you make a trust move? Not from a career to a marriage but from your way to God's way."

"Everyone take out your index card and grab a pen," Anne said suddenly. "I think it would be good for each of us in turn to scratch out the obstacle we've written down on our card and write underneath it one bold move we could make as a first step to becoming a New Eve."

"That's a good idea!" Brenda exclaimed. "And we can help each other think of what to say."

The room grew silent for a few moments. Susan tapped her card with her pen and then wrote something down. "Anne," she said, "here's my bold move."

> ~~In career I trust.~~
> *Entrust my life to a biblical definition of womanhood, especially the "chooses wisely" part.*

"That's the heart of the issue with me. I'm not comfortable with where my choices have been taking me. I saw my mom's life get wrecked in marriage and I've run from that and tried to establish some kind of career self-sufficiency. Now I'm thinking, *Have I hardened myself against courageously pursuing some of the callings God has for me?* Maybe so. I've got some thinking to do."

◆

The ladies then discussed how they could help each other process their bold moves over the next few months. After they had nailed down a plan, Anne spoke up.

"I want to follow up on some things Patricia said about her situation. You say you're afraid you've missed out on the good life, but I want to affirm how I've seen you be a godly example. For instance, I was amazed at the ministry you had with those inner-city kids at the community center this summer. You were an incredible leader and a huge asset in making that project a success. Also, I saw how you poured your heart out to the children you personally worked with."

"Thank you, Anne! That's sweet of you. Your encouragement brings to mind the need to say how good God has been to me. I do think I've made some unwise choices, and that has cost me some of the good things I might have enjoyed in life. But all the same, God has provided me with many opportunities and blessings that are probably exclusive to single gals."

She laughed in an easy manner and then continued. "It's like this: my time and my money are my own. There are no conditions on either of them. I'm able to use my resources to impact the lives of others. I've traveled the world. Sometimes for fun, sometimes for work, but I've learned that I can take the gospel with me in word and deed no matter where I am. And I've had some wonderful experiences doing so. Besides, as you all know, I was able to pick up and move here last year from Chicago so I could take care of my ailing sister. I couldn't have done that if I were married. So God has good, life-giving purposes even for us single gals! The trick is keeping that in perspective during the lonely times."

"So what's your bold move?" Brenda asked after a brief pause. Patricia scratched a sentence onto her card and held it up for the ladies.

> ~~Did I miss the good life?~~
> *To live with the end in mind.*

"Now more than ever, I need to define and be clear about the kind of life God wants me to live before my time here is up. I don't want to miss anything He has out there for me. If I keep that kind of life in focus, I think I'll be better able to navigate this second half of my life and maximize it. In this way I'll also be able to experience the good things God still has for me. I've made some mistakes I've regretted, but that's over!"

◆

"What about you, Brenda?" Susan asked. "What's your biggest struggle with living out the biblical ideals for womanhood?"

Brenda looked down at her card. Her worried hands had bent and folded it many times until its ragged appearance matched her spirit. Realizing this, she folded it deeper into her palm, hiding it for a moment. It was her card, her pain.

"Here's what I wrote," she finally said, her voice breaking a little as she unfolded her card for all to see.

I've lost hope
for my marriage.

The group sat in silence. This was a raw moment. Brenda considered her next words carefully. Anne flashed a prayer through her mind.

"The struggles I'm facing began long ago," Brenda said. "My home was a wreck growing up. Mom and Dad fought all the time before Dad left for good when I was five. That hurt so bad. Still does. In some sense the rest of my life has been defined by that.

"As a teen, I fell for every guy who showed interest in me. Even if I knew better, knew his character was bad, I would find myself quickly pulled into a relationship. And it was always physical. I *so* wanted somebody, and I thought this was the way you made it happen."

Brenda then shared about teenage relationships that started bad and finished worse. She talked about disappointment, pain, and consequences. She even talked about abortion. She'd secretly had one in a big-city clinic before her twentieth birthday. And even though she'd confessed it to God, she had never forgiven herself.

"My first marriage was about sex and impulse—mostly impulse. You can imagine how that ended. We had a couple of kids straight out of the gate and never synced up on anything. It was total war. We both worked full-time and kept separate circles of friends. Then he started drinking heavily. I put up with it awhile, but when I discovered his other woman, I took the kids and drove until we stopped here in Raleigh. I didn't know anyone. I just needed a new start in a new town where I could disappear and lick my wounds in peace.

"That's when I became a Christian. At my lowest point a stranger talked to me about Jesus, and I believed with everything in me. What happened next was amazing and in many ways freeing. I discovered a new life, made new friends, and found this church, which has been incredibly supportive. Unfortunately, I still didn't know a thing about men. The needs inside me that had driven me recklessly from man to man were still unaddressed. So I continued to bounce around from one bad relationship to the next.

"Finally, I met John. I met him here at church actually. I knew he was the one early on, but we waited awhile so I could prove to myself I wasn't being impulsive again. But look at us, we're a mess anyway," she said, dabbing tears from her eyes. "I love John and I know he loves me, but there's friction that I really don't understand. I think a lot of the problem is that he won't take charge of the situation. We come to church and we're involved in a small group. But I can't get him to take the initiative in our relationship. It's like he just comes home and retreats to his little world in front of the TV.

"I wish he could be more like some of the men I see at church every Sunday. They're spiritual leaders who seem eager to take on their responsibilities. But I can't get John to do any of those things!"

"What are some of the good things about your husband, Brenda?" Anne wanted to know. "What is he doing well for you and the kids?"

Brenda looked as if she'd been asked to name the secretary to the third president of the United States. "That's funny," she said, "I . . . I haven't thought of that in a while. I guess I can't say off the top of my head."

"Does he earn a regular paycheck?"

"Sure. He hasn't had a sick day in five years."

"Has he been faithful to your marriage? Is he good to the kids?"

"Yeah, he's steady on those things. Nothing spectacular, but steady." Brenda started to smile. "I think I'm getting the point. I've locked in on the negative, haven't I?"

"Anybody can make that mistake," said Anne. "But it's easy to correct. What might not be as easy is for you to seek outside help for your marriage. Maybe you could start by asking another woman who *is* happily married to mentor you for a time. Or maybe you need personal counseling to explore your past and how it might be affecting your relationship with John and how you relate to him. At some point John might join you in that process to develop together some new patterns of relating. The point is, you need to stop *reacting* to John and start exploring some new ways to *engage* him."

After talking it over for a minute, Brenda got out her battered little card. "I guess it's kind of obvious what my bold move should be." She scribbled it down quickly.

> ~~I've lost hope for my marriage.~~
> I need to use wisdom
> with my man.

"That's a wonderful first step!" declared Anne. "And that's something you can do right now."

◆

When the discussion about Brenda's situation quieted down, Tracey took the initiative and waved her card vigorously in the air for all to see.

> *I feel left out.*

"Not here, of course. I don't feel left out here. But sometimes I do feel left out of the larger world. I hear people talk about their careers and I can't relate at all. It's not that I have it bad or anything. Far from it. My husband has a pretty good job, so we're making it OK. Besides, I love my family and I know I'm doing important work at home. But I've never tasted what it's like to have a career and prove myself as a professional. I got married the summer before my senior year of college and had my first child a few months after graduation, so I never established the outside-the-home credibility all my friends seem to have. Even my younger sister, who I practically raised, knows more than I do about what it takes to make it out there. It all makes me feel second-class. Does that seem silly?"

"Not at all," said Brenda. "A lot of stay-at-home moms feel that way."

"Absolutely. Absolutely!" said Anne. "I often struggled with that when I was on my knees before a cruddy toilet or as I washed the same dish for the ten-thousandth time. So many of the things we do to care for a household can seem menial and mindless. It's easy to feel second-class and insignificant, especially with young kids like yours."

"Yes!" said Tracey. "Thanks for affirming that."

"The flip side to all of this," Patricia reminded her, "is that all those things your career-oriented friends have are not half as life-giving as you're tempted to think. This is a worn-out cliché but it's as true as ever: Money doesn't buy happiness. Trust me. The women out there who seem to you to have it all have their own struggles, worse than you'd guess in many cases. Many dream of a life like yours."

"I believe that," said Tracey. "I lose sight of it sometimes, but I really do believe that. It's so easy to look out there in the world and start comparing myself to every girl in a business suit and a glamorous home." She pulled out her card and a pen as she said this, then showed the ladies her bold move.

> ~~I feel left out.~~
> *Live from the inside out.*

"If I can do that and not pay so much attention to the values and images of the world, I know I'll be more at peace. I know what I'm doing is right. I just want to *feel* it."

"And keep this in mind," added Anne. "You have a college degree. There's no use letting it die a slow death at the hands of negligence. What was your major?"

"Interior decorating," Tracey answered. "I loved every minute of it."

"Good! Why not stay updated in your field by reading magazines, browsing stores, and occasionally going to trade shows? And when a friend wants to redecorate, offer your services. You can do it part-time while your kids are small and then maybe add more work as they get older. I know this is a busy season of life for you, but it wouldn't take much to keep yourself sharp. And the payoff in the future will be worth the effort."

Tracey waved her card again and said, "That's very doable and exciting. Thanks!"

◆

All eyes now turned to Anne. Everyone half expected to see Anne reveal a perfectly blank card. After all, her acts of service were known to everyone in the church and the community, and her smile could cheer any soul. What could a godly woman like Anne be struggling with? Here was a New Eve if ever there was one.

"It's real simple for me," said Anne. "On the whole I've had a good life so far. I'm satisfied that I made more good choices than bad ones, primarily because of God's Word and God's grace. My husband and children are doing well, and nothing makes me happier than that. But what now? What do I do with my life now that the kids are all gone? So here's my card."

What's next for me?

"When I was younger, I imagined fifty-six was ancient, the end of the road. You'd be nestled down in a rocking chair somewhere with yarn and knitting needles and wouldn't look up until they came for your body. But what I'm finding now is that fifty-six is *young*. I've got probably thirty years or so ahead of me! I'm not designed to just fold my cards and wait out my time. No one is. So my challenge is figuring out what I'm supposed to do with the rest of my life."

"What sort of work did you do before marriage and kids?" asked Patricia.

"Catering. I helped cater weddings, birthdays, graduations . . . even the inauguration of Governor Jameson. I was the first assistant to Mrs. Carter at Carter Catering. It was a great experience."

"That explains this," Brenda said, motioning to the table laden with Anne's preparations. "You've got a real talent there, Anne."

"Any thought of getting back into that?" Tracey asked. "Take the advice you just gave me?"

"Well, sure. I suppose I think of that some. It's a funny thing, though. Having spent the past twenty-nine years putting all my energies into my family, I've lost a little bit of the initiative for getting out there and doing my work for the public. I'm not sure how it's come to be this way, but new challenges are a little frightening to me now."

"Start small," Patricia said matter-of-factly. "Start small, get comfortable, then deepen your involvement as you get your legs under you."

"Before long you'll be back doing inaugurations!" declared Susan. "And I'll bet I can get you to cater some of the conferences we do at work. You'd be a big hit, Anne."

"They're right, Anne," said Brenda. "It's time to relaunch and explore the new opportunities for you. And I have another idea. Instead of focusing on starting a new business, which I know you'd do great at, you could pour your energies into helping feed the needy. I know there are homeless shelters and other non-profits that would love to have you aboard. Think of the impact you could make!"

This set all the ladies to talking about the range of possibilities for Anne. Everyone agreed she had many great options to consider since she so obviously enjoyed serving others. Anne wrote as she listened and then flashed her card for all to see.

"It's a new day!" Anne declared with a smile. "And a great time to find a new purpose in life."

> ~~What's next for me?~~
> Adopt the "big-picture" perspective and enthusiastically embrace my new season of life.

Conclusion

As you can see from the previous stories, being a New Eve is not about a static, cookie-cutter, one-for-all lifestyle. It's about you being *you!* God's you. The best you. It's about leaps of faith, bold moves, and deep convictions that refuse to be swayed by the world. It's also about finding and securing the life you've always wanted, a good life without regrets.

Unfortunately, the first Eve came to believe that the best way to have that kind of life was by rejecting God, ignoring His command, and reaching for a glitzier something else. This became the tragic bold move that marked not only her life but also the lives of many millions of Eves since. The New Eve is a woman precisely as daring, except in the opposite way. Her distinction is in the way she tenaciously holds on to God's design and callings as radically as the first Eve abandoned hers. This is the proven path to a rewarding life.

So where do you start? The women in this chapter did a smart thing. They started their New Eve journeys by asking two questions to give them both a focus and a first step: What is life's biggest challenge for me right now? and What should be my first bold move? If you deeply desire a life that pleases God, that's a good starting place for you too. It's always better to start small and build on a few successes than it is to try too much all at once and then give up.

So what is your biggest challenge as a woman?

And what will be your first bold move as a New Eve?

Bold Femininity

Live from the Inside Out

Adopt a Biblical Definition of Womanhood

Embrace a Big-Picture Perspective on Life

Live with the End in Mind

Use Wisdom with a Man

The New Eve

Postscript

How You and Your Family Shape the Future

I originally intended for this material to be included as a chapter in The New Eve. However, it soon became apparent that it did not fit the more practical nature of the book, and so it was dropped. I choose to include it here for those of you who may be interested in venturing out into the "deeper" sociological waters of the role family plays in how people and cultures rise and fall.

Marriage and family matter for a lot of reasons: personal fulfillment, loving companionship, raising children, redeeming society, preserving culture, saving civilization, and altering history.

Say what?

You heard me right. The reach of marriage and family extends well beyond our personal needs and wants. It was designed to do far more than merely make us happy. Look back at Genesis, which outlines the blueprints for marriage. Certainly God intended marriage to meet our aloneness needs (Gen. 2:18), but

He also intended it to be a tightly knit, peaceful "battle group" that goes forth to subdue the earth with godly order (Gen. 1:28). Every time a family succeeds in that mission, society is empowered and social order is advanced. Conversely, every time one fails, society is wounded and social order, in one way or another, breaks down.

Marriage and family are that important.

A New Eve knows that. It's a conviction that runs deep within her. She understands that what goes on in her home has a wide range of impacts. By expressing godly values and releasing healthy children, she can change a neighborhood, a city, a state, a nation, or even the world. This is the great, inspiring vision that Genesis casts for marriage and that a New Eve embraces for herself on a personal level. She is right in believing that her home represents nothing less than the future of the world.

What History Has to Say

History proves that marriage is a social and spiritual megaforce that shapes whole nations one couple at a time. Nations rise and fall, excel and decline, and wax and wane based on the state of their marriages.

In 1947, long before marriage was a controversial subject, Dr. Carle Zimmerman of Harvard University wrote an insightful book called *Family and Civilization*. The goal of his exhaustive research was to discover the impact of different marriage and family models on the state of a civilization. Was there any specific correlation between a nation's fitness—its economic and social well-being—and its family patterns? That was the question at the heart of Zimmerman's study. To find the answer, he examined the institution of marriage across time and culture. He discovered that civilized nations all begin by manifesting one type of family structure, thrive as a second type dominates, and then inevitably decline under a third model. In other words, he demonstrated a direct correlation between specific family types and the rise and fall of cultures. Some marriage and family models help build empires and nations; others help kill them.

Here, then, are the three family patterns Zimmerman found that marked the life cycle of a civilization.

The Trustee Family

The trustee model predominates in the early stages of civilization. Zimmerman called it "trustee" because each member of the family, from the young daughter cutting her teeth to the shriveled grandfather who has long since lost his, is *entrusted* with the responsibility of preserving family life and family values. Individual freedoms and personal rights are rare. It's a kin-and-clan-first mentality, and the family members are judged by how well they bear this value out in their choices and actions. Today emerging countries in Africa and the Middle East are marked more or less by this family model.

The trustee family is patriarchal in structure, with men enjoying wide-ranging power over women and children. That power, however, is not arbitrary but is an expression of the will of a larger clan to which the family belongs. Men don't simply make the rules up as they go. They must follow the accepted practices and values of clan life, and this includes protections for the rights and well-being of women and children. Nevertheless, the dominant male is permitted to lead by strength or even physical aggression when members stray from the distinct roles given them.

Societies embrace the trustee model early in their life cycle because it's necessitated by their underdeveloped context. Conditions are difficult at this stage of society. In order for a family to eat and live in security, each family member has to give selflessly to the team effort. Resources must be hunted, farmed, or mined from the land. All of this requires a no-nonsense approach to life that is pragmatic and productive. Children are seen as an asset—there's plenty they can do in the fields and around the house to help move the family forward. Women play the vital roles of feeding and clothing the family, working in and around the home, as well as adding new members through childbirth. Men, with their strong backs and aggressive bent, work to provide for the family's needs, as well as man the battle lines.

In these conditions there's no time for philosophizing on the larger questions of how gender equality and children's rights might play themselves out in a fully equitable society. Nor is society advanced enough to put forth a strong governing body that can craft and enforce these kinds of civil laws. Thus, clans enforce their own laws for behavior. Tribal rule prevails. However, as the trustee model gradually succeeds in helping society tame the land, develop technologies, and grow in numbers, a more advanced and equitable model of the family appears.

The Domestic Family

In this family type a husband and wife come together to form a new, more autonomous unity. Both partners retain significant links to the larger clan, but their lifestyle decisions are no longer dictated by its rules and values. No more family councils. No more decisions handed down from the clan hierarchy. Individual families rule themselves, guided by the strong religious and family-centric values that predominate during this phase of society. This is the pro-family era of civilization.

Personal freedoms begin to emerge among family members. Roles are still important and well defined for each member in the family, but they're more flexible than was the case in the trustee model. Family unity is still a value freely embraced, but it is no longer a law to be enforced. In all but aberrant cases, every family member is highly valued. Neither gender nor age can diminish one's worth. Even still, there remains a noteworthy division of labor along gender lines, with women seeing to the needs of the home and men focusing outward. But there's also a new sharing of domestic and workplace responsibilities that was not seen in the trustee model. This is not only the result of a shift from subsistence living to a more comfortable lifestyle filled with conveniences and free time; it also reflects new values. For instance, women and children have more legal and personal rights under this model.

The husband is still the head of the household, but in a way that is now more benevolent than authoritarian. Laws and social expectations increasingly discourage him from exerting the sort of heavy-handed domination that could be sanctioned in the trustee model. He's the team captain rather than the boss. He leads rather than demands, and it's his duty to serve the needs of his entire family. In many ways America adopted this form of family early in its development and then lived by it until well into the twentieth century.

Zimmerman identified the domestic family model as the one under which a society becomes most creative.[1] Building, growing, inventing, discovering, and expanding horizons—when the family is hitting on all cylinders, drawing on the powers and dignity that each member can bring to domestic and societal goals, the nation powers toward its zenith of achievement. Ancient Greece and Rome, as well as modern Europe and America, could all be cited as examples of cultures that experienced extraordinary success under this domestic-family model. But like most good things, history shows it doesn't last. Just when the domestic model is most prominent, society begins to shift once again.

The Atomistic Family

The word *atomistic* refers to the breaking up of the whole into "atoms" or individual parts. Hence, the atomistic family is one in which the fundamental unity of man and wife, parent and child, is eventually shattered by invasive social and personal forces that place greater emphasis on individual expression and personal freedoms than on adherence to traditional family bonds. Furthermore, the broad religious consensus that previously guided the domestic society unravels in an increasingly atomistic age. Before long the individual trumps the family. Universal beliefs that held people and families together in the past dissolve into individual beliefs that push them apart. In short, the unifying forces of family and religion slowly become extinct during this atomistic phase of culture.

The last bastions of gender inequality that survived the reforms of the domestic era are addressed as society now seeks to liberate and equalize all individuals. Unfortunately, these good measures are accompanied by a misguided philosophy that holds that unchecked personal freedom is the highest goal of society. The atomistic era shuns religion and traditional family structures and is fueled by the belief that people are capable of living productive lives in whatever ways they choose.

Zimmerman found that as the atomistic way of life spreads within a culture, lines of authority flatten out. An unqualified sameness takes hold between the sexes and even between parents and children. With all members more and more focused on themselves, what was previously known as "family" slowly destabilizes and loses its sense of cohesion. And when families—the very backbone of a nation and its culture—lack cohesion, soon the nation itself begins to unravel and slowly drown in its own toxic self-absorption. It happened in Greece. It happened in Rome. There is strong evidence that it is happening today throughout the Western world.

In summary, Zimmerman discovered in his research that family types and cultural life and death are directly related to one another. Indeed, you can mark where a nation is in its life cycle by the kind of family model that dominates its cultural landscape.

Today's Landscape

So where are we today? Interestingly, in 1947 Zimmerman believed America was already transitioning into the atomistic era. With history as his guide, he outlined in his book what he believed our culture would increasingly look like as atomism took hold of succeeding American generations. Here are the six specific characteristics that Zimmerman envisioned for a future America.

1. Marriage loses its sacredness and is increasingly broken by divorce.

In the atomistic age marriage is no longer protected by strict laws, deep religious beliefs, social pressures, or a strong "we-will-make-it-work" attitude. Instead, moving out of marriage comes to be seen not as a failure but as a no-fault right. Predictably, as the barriers for leaving a marriage are lowered, so are the personal commitments required for entering it. The result is a "dumbed down" version of what was once a "till-death-do-us-part" covenant. In the atomistic age marriage has very little staying power.

2. Alternate forms of marriage arise and supplant traditional marriage agreements.

I once talked to a young groom-to-be who was bragging that he was going about marriage the modern way: by getting a prenuptial agreement. I told him there was nothing modern about it. The Romans were doing it in the time of Christ. They also sanctioned gay unions. Nothing new there either. But it's important to remember that Rome was not always that way. Rome and other empires were built on the traditional form of marriage. Only after a time of development and prosperity did they choose to relax and broaden the meaning of marriage, as we are now considering in America.

If history tells us anything, it's that once the meaning of marriage is redefined beyond the traditional one-man, one-woman arrangement, almost any union of people eventually finds legal sanction. Stanley Kurtz, a scholar of the forms and roles of marriage in contemporary society, said there is a growing push among lawmakers to "establish the principle that individuals have the right to create and define their families as they see fit." This will no doubt include the right to take multiple wives and even marry underage girls. Kurtz went on to say that the acceptance of same-sex marriage may spell "the effective abolition of marriage itself as a legal status."[2]

3. Feminist movements arise. Women lose their inclination for childbearing and child rearing. Birthrates fall.

The loosening of family and marital ties is accompanied and empowered by feminist movements. I'm not talking about the fight for gender equality—a fight we should all support. By feminism I mean the more radical movement that leads women to minimize or reject elements of their God-given feminine nature. One of the clearest ways this manifests itself is in the growing disinclination to bear and raise children.

This reality is on display in contemporary Europe and America right now. As mentioned earlier in this book, robust immigration (legal and otherwise) is the only reason the U.S. population continues to grow. Shut down the borders, and we'd find America at a population standstill. It is much more serious in many parts of Europe, where women's disdain for childbirth is a mark of their liberation from the villainized domestic-family model. Many European countries are in a population freefall that reminds me of ancient Rome.

When liberated Roman women stopped having babies and Roman men ditched their family and social responsibilities, the so-called barbarian immigrants from northern Europe came and filled the void. They served in the armies, they performed the labors, and they bore the children. It was the noncitizen barbarian, said Zimmerman, who in many ways kept the empire going for three centuries after Roman citizens sacrificed their future by giving up on marriage and family.

Zimmerman concluded his book by warning that America is falling into this same trap. He anticipated that America, like Rome, would be threatened by an increasingly comfort-driven lifestyle that is prone less and less to procreate and trusts in immigration to do the dirty work and fill the voids. He even suggested that one day we would have to turn to Mexico for a quick fix of surplus population. But, he warned, to trust in immigration is nothing more than a delay tactic before one's own cultural demise. If we ignore our God-given calling to repopulate and to build healthy marriages and families, it will prove disastrous.

As Zimmerman concluded, he reminded readers that *"family and childbearing are the primary social duties of the citizen."*[3] What Zimmerman ended with, Genesis begins with.

4. Destructive juvenile behavior increases.

Zimmerman also noted that the atomistic model engenders a growing disrespect for parental authority and for authority in general. It's tempting to pin this on the kids or society, but the fact is, it's the parents who are mostly to blame. When parents work too long, play too much, and refuse to do the hard duties of parenting, kids become love-deprived, lack development in many basic life skills, and feel emotionally abandoned. Understandably, this parental negligence soon adds up to anger, rebellion, and license in the hearts of children. The inevitable result is an increase in juvenile delinquency, teenage violence, crime, drug addiction, and promiscuity. As sociological data firmly indicate, these realities of the atomistic age increasingly mark our culture.

5. There is a growing disregard for family responsibilities.

One of the signal traits of the trustee and domestic models is that everyone in the family has a clear set of responsibilities to fulfill. They don't seriously question them. They won't always enjoy the assignments that fall to them, but they fulfill their obligations because they know a lot is riding on their shoulders.

In the atomistic model this sense of responsibility is slowly replaced by a demand for liberation. Family members want to share in the prosperities of family life but not the duties. You've seen examples of this on TV. A mom asks her son to make up his bed, and all he can manage to do is yell back, "Hire someone to do that, Mom!"

6. There is an increasing desire for and acceptance of adultery, as well as a greater tolerance for sexual expressions of all kinds.

Finally, the atomization of society means unleashing a sexuality that is entirely unbounded. Growing sexual immorality and deepening sexual perversions seem to go hand in hand with the unraveling of family life. In many cases these sexual excesses are a twisted attempt to recapture the love missed in childhood.

The atomistic society feels entitled to open the door to sexual expressions of every kind. Extreme forms of immorality are not only justified but also celebrated. This drift into decadence isn't new. History has seen it many times before. But for us, it signals the arrival of the atomistic age.

What Does It All Mean?

In his classic book *Lord of the Flies*, William Golding portrayed a group of British prep-school boys stranded on an uncharted island. Cut off from adult supervision, the boys realize it is up to them to organize a makeshift society. "We've got to have rules and obey them. After all, we're not savages," says one of the boys early in the misadventure.[4]

But base savagery is the very thing the boys quickly adopt. Far from duplicating the manner-minded English society of their parents, the boys create a new order based on raw power and savagery. They bicker, belittle, fight, and even kill each other for control.

From mannered to mad in no time flat. How is that possible? The answer is this: the well-ordered home is the centerpiece of a civilized society. Without the parent-to-child transference of wisdom, restraint, and moral fiber, humans tend toward barbarism. It's a part of our fallen condition. We're always one generation away from savagery, but we don't believe it until reality kicks down the door. Good homes are the only antidote. That's why your marriage is so important. It carries the future of our country. It also carries the future of God's kingdom work here on Earth.

The Biblical Family

It's important to recognize that despite Zimmerman's helpful research on family models, *none* of his models adequately describes what Scripture sets forth as "the biblical family." (For a more detailed discussion of the biblical family, I suggest you read my book, *Rocking the Roles: Building a Win-Win Marriage*, published by NavPress.)

Compared to the biblical model, the trustee family is heavy-handed, overly patriarchal, and for everyone besides the head male, too confining. The domestic-family model, on the other hand, comes closer to the biblical outline in its application. But the domestic family is *not* the biblical model either. It, too, falls short in many ways, especially when it comes to offering wives the full equality of status and opportunity the Bible says women deserve in marriage (1 Pet. 3:7) and pressing husbands to shoulder a more balanced share of the relational, social, and spiritual responsibilities of the family (Deut. 6:6–7; Ps. 78:5–7; Eph. 5:25, 6:4). Lastly, compared to the biblical family, the atomistic model is far too loose, too self-centered, and too irresponsible to be compatible with God's design for family.

All this to say, the Bible endorses none of the above family models. Instead it sets forth its own set of unique blueprints (outlined in chap. 11) for what the family should look like to please God. When followed in faith and everyday practice, the biblical model for family will help ensure the health and development of each member of the family. This in turn will positively shape our larger culture. That's why a New Eve embraces these biblical blueprints and builds her home on them.

Conclusion

A New Eve recognizes that her family is a crucial change agent within society. She knows her family has been designed by God to be a redemptive force for good, regardless of the age in which she lives, even an atomistic one. That means you and your family can be a part of restoring our nation to health. *Believe it!* Even an atomized society can be reunified. But it has to happen one family at a time. A New Eve carries that conviction deep in her heart and allows it to shape her pursuits and priorities. She knows what God knows: her family is society's future.

Small-Group
Study Guide
and Discussion Questions

1. Introduction

The following study guide with small-group discussion questions is provided to help you join with a small group of women to process and personalize the insights and challenges found in *The New Eve*.

Small groups work best when the group size allows everyone the opportunity to freely participate. It is recommended that your group be no larger than five or six in number. One woman should serve as the moderator with the following responsibilities:

- To provide a setting that is comfortable and free of interruption
- To establish and maintain starting and stopping times
- To facilitate the weekly discussions, making sure everyone participates
- To keep everyone informed of the weekly assignments
- To encourage prayer for one another

2. Select the Type of Small Group You Want

Several types of small groups can be formed around *The New Eve*:

- The *eclectic* small group, made up of adult women of all ages, preferably led by a mature Christian woman.
- The *age-specific* small group, made up of women in a common season of life. For help on the seasons of life, see chapters 7 and 8. If the small group is composed specifically of younger women (twenties and/or thirties in age), it is highly recommended that one or two more experienced mentors facilitate the group.
- The *mother-daughter* small group. This group works best when all the daughters participating are between the ages of eighteen and twenty. This gives the moms a great opportunity to "initiate" their daughters into the specifics of Christian womanhood at a crucial developmental period of their lives. In such cases, some kind of special ceremony calling these young daughters to pursue bold, godly femininity might be a fitting way to end this study.

3. The Nine Discussion Sessions

Nine New Eve discussion sessions cover the twelve chapters in this book. Six of these sessions focus on single chapters. Three cover two chapters each. The final discussion session focuses specifically on each participant's personal takeaways and the one bold move each woman plans to concentrate on once the study has concluded.

Two additional resources are available to enhance this study. First is a **Discussion Starter DVD,** which is available to help you launch each of your small group discussions. In this video, Dr. Robert Lewis and his host, Lisa Fischer, open both the orientation meeting and each of the nine discussion sessions to you in a more personal way. Their comments are designed to give focus and added energy to the beginning of each of your small-group times.

Second, a recording of a live presentation of *The New Eve* by Dr. Lewis is available on CD for you to listen to. This can be used after your study has concluded as an easy way to review the New Eve material and reinforce key insights you have learned. Both the CD package and the Discussion Starter DVD can be obtained by calling Fellowship Associates at 1-800-446-7228 or by going online at www.mensfraternity.com.

4. Begin with an Orientation Meeting

Small-group discussions work best when group participants know one another and the ground rules for meeting together. Therefore, once a small group of women has expressed interest in doing a New Eve study together and a leader has been identified, a preparatory meeting should be arranged to help the group get started right.

At this relaxed orientation meeting, the group leader allows whatever time is necessary for group members to comfortably get to know one another and invites each woman to tell the group what she hopes to receive from this study. The leader should also allow Robert Lewis and Lisa Fischer to introduce themselves by showing the group the first Discussion Starter video.

After these introductions the leader should remind the women that the focus of this study will be to offer each woman in the group specific, hands-on ways of making her unique life better, richer, more meaningful, and more honoring to God. At its best this New Eve study and discussion should provide time for thought-provoking interaction and reflection, personal examination, and helpful life-changing applications.

With that said, the leader will work through the following checklist with the group members:

- Set a place and date for the first meeting.
- Gain a commitment from each woman to attend all nine discussion sessions.
- Set starting and stopping times for each of the small-group discussions.
- Establish the "golden rule" of small-group discussion: everyone will participate, and no one will dominate.
- Make time (five minutes or more) for reflection at the end of every small-group discussion time for group members to write specific applications (new beliefs, priorities, behavior, ways of thinking, etc.) for themselves that would make life better.
- Make sure everyone has a book and knows to read chapter 1 and to work through the discussion questions before the first meeting.

Session 1
Discussion Questions

Chapters 1 and 2

Writing out your initial answers to these questions *before* your small-group meeting will enhance the quality of your discussions. Take a moment to record your answers.

1. Chapter 1 captures some of the immense sociological changes that have unfolded in and around the lives of modern women. How have these changes impacted and influenced your life?

2. Are there specific changes happening to women today that concern you? What are they, and why do they concern you?

3. True or false: Women can have it all. Explain your answer.

4. What does a successful and fulfilling life look like to you as a woman right now? Can you describe it in specific terms?

5. Given so many new freedoms today, what would you think are the biggest trouble spots for women to look out for? Where have you made mistakes?

6. In this new world of opportunity, do you personally have clear guidelines for navigating life successfully? If so, what are they? If not, what do you think you need?

7. Chapter 2 presents four general worldviews or mind-sets women (and men) may live from. Which of these four worldviews do you think best describes how you live your life? Explain your answer.

8. Look over the five bold moves introduced at the end of this chapter. Which one grabs your attention the most here at the start? Tell why.

Post-discussion Takeaways

Now that you have read these chapters and had your discussion time, what personal applications (new beliefs, priorities, behaviors, ways of thinking, etc.) will you leave with? Take a few minutes and record them in the space below.

Session 2
Discussion Questions

Chapter 3

Writing out your initial answers to these questions *before* your small-group meeting will enhance the quality of your discussions. Take a moment to record your answers.

1. Look over the list provided in this chapter of problems women say they struggle with. Which ones did you circle that personally apply to your life? Explain. Can you spot a common theme to the problems you've circled? If so, what is it?

2. This chapter focuses on five major issues swirling around the lives of women today. How would you rank them in order of importance and impact on your life, with 1 being most important and 5 being least important?

_____ An ever-evolving femininity

_____ A new supreme pursuit

_____ The challenge of motherhood

_____ Successfully engaging a man

_____ The maze of unlimited choices

Tell why you ranked these issues the way you did. Do the common problems you discerned for your life from question #1 fit into one of the five issues?

3. As you look over these five major issues, what important questions do they raise for you personally that you would pay money to have answered?

4. Where are you on the "swinging social pendulum" of evolving femininity? Are you still in a traditional role? The do-it-all role? The sameness role? Role reversal? Explain. What role would you design for yourself if you could do so right now?

5. Looking back, have you been disappointed with some of your choices in life? Which one stands out? What led you to believe at the time this choice was a good one? What could have helped you to make a better decision, knowing what you know now?

6. What was your greatest personal insight from this chapter? Explain.

7. What is one thing you would like the other women in the group to pray with you about?

Post-discussion Takeaways

Now that you have read this chapter and had your discussion time, what personal applications (new beliefs, priorities, behaviors, ways of thinking, etc.) will you leave with? Take a few minutes and record them in the space below.

Session 3
Discussion Questions

Chapters 4 and 5

Writing out your initial answers to these questions *before* your small-group meeting will enhance the quality of your discussions. Take a moment to record your answers.

1. Chapters 4 and 5 assume that the Genesis account of creation is foundational to understanding God's timeless design for gender. Is that your assumption? Why or why not? How much weight do you give Genesis in shaping your life as a woman? A little? A lot? None? Not sure? Pick one and tell why.

2. In reading about the core callings of every woman in chapter 4, did you feel excited, disturbed, relieved, challenged, or something else? Share your thoughts with the group.

3. What conclusions is Genesis drawing for you concerning the purpose of your life as a woman? The priorities of your life as a woman? The kind of freedom you have as a woman? The way to go about making choices as a woman? Take some time on this question.

4. Which direction of life is most impacting you right now: living from the outside in or living from the inside out? Explain your answer.

5. If you took the bold move of living from the inside out more seriously, how would it alter your life as a woman? In what specific ways? What would hold you back from taking that step? Explain.

6. What important warnings does the life of Eve offer modern women today? Share as a group as many as you can.

7. What impacted you the most from these two chapters and this discussion? What questions or concerns do you still have?

Post-discussion Takeaways

Now that you have read these chapters and had your discussion time, what personal applications (new beliefs, priorities, behaviors, ways of thinking, etc.) will you leave with? Take a few minutes and record them in the space below.

Session 4
Discussion Questions

Chapter 6

Writing out your initial answers to these questions *before* your small-group meeting will enhance the quality of your discussions. Take a moment to record your answers.

1. This chapter begins with the statement "Vision energizes life." Before this study began, what vision of womanhood (if any) has been calling your life forward? Can you describe it? How did you decide on that particular vision? What was the source of it?

2. Share your thoughts concerning the biblical definition of manhood presented in this chapter. What specific aspects of this manhood definition are you drawn to? What aspects are you less certain about? Explain.

3. How did you feel about using Eve and Mary as the main characters for constructing a biblical definition of womanhood? Explain.

4. This chapter makes three comparisons between Eve and Mary. What did you find in these comparisons that could be applied to your life?

5. Share your thoughts on the biblical definition of womanhood presented in this chapter. Is it helpful? How? What reservations (if any) do you have with it?

6. Which of the four parts of the biblical definition of womanhood is most meaningful to you? Tell why.

7. The second bold move of a New Eve is to adopt a biblical definition of womanhood. Can you adopt the definition given in this chapter for your life? Would you have a passion to pass it on to others? To your daughters? Why or why not? If not, what definition of womanhood will you use to call your life forward?

8. What was the most influential thing you learned from this chapter? Explain.

Post-discussion Takeaways

Now that you have read this chapter and had your discussion time, what personal applications (new beliefs, priorities, behaviors, ways of thinking, etc.) will you leave with? Take a few minutes and record them in the space below.

Session 5
Discussion Questions

Chapters 7 and 8

Writing out your initial answers to these questions *before* your small-group meeting will enhance the quality of your discussions. Take a moment to record your answers.

1. The third bold move of a New Eve is to embrace a big-picture perspective on life. How do you see that helping a woman manage her life? What mistakes (if any) have you made by having a shortsighted perspective? Explain.

2. React to Sylvia Ann Hewlett's advice to young women found in chapter 7. Agree or disagree? Give reasons for your answer.

3. Pick a season of life you have already lived through. Does the wisdom being offered for that season in these chapters fit what you learned, having gone through it? What would you change? What would you add?

4. Look at the wisdom offered in the season of life you are now in. What is there that affirms you? What challenges you? What are you not sure of or not clear about? Ask any woman in the group who has already passed through your present season to share her thoughts and insights with you.

5. Look at the season that comes next in your life. What are you doing now that will make the transition to this next season go smoothly? What are you doing now that might make this next season harder?

6. If you have had to blend two seasons into one (and many women do), what wise moves would you include in this new blend? Explain. What advice could the other members of your small group offer you?

7. Look as a group at the final season of a woman's life: the Glorified Saint. What do you feel about your life now as you read through this last season? What helpful insights does it offer you?

8. After discussing these chapters, what is one thing you could do now to live better as a woman from this big-picture perspective? Explain.

Post-discussion Takeaways

Now that you have read these chapters and had your discussion time, what personal applications (new beliefs, priorities, behaviors, ways of thinking, etc.) will you leave with? Take a few minutes and record them in the space below.

Note: Please come to the next session with one or two end goals filled out in your "Before I die, I want to . . ." diagram at the end of chapter 9. This will be *very important* for your next small-group discussion.

Session 6
Discussion Questions

Chapter 9

Writing out your initial answers to these questions *before* your small-group meeting will enhance the quality of your discussions. Take a moment to record your answers.

1. "Thinking ahead" and "Knowing where you're going"—where have you seen the wisdom of these statements proved in your life? Explain. Where have you made mistakes and wasted time and opportunities by not heeding such wisdom?

2. Share your thoughts on the fourth bold move of a New Eve: Live with the end in mind. On a scale of 1 to 5, with 5 being very clear and 1 being totally unclear, how well would you say you've defined your end? Explain.

3. Before now have you ever written down your end goals? If so, has that worked for you? What have been the benefits?

4. Look again at Ephesians 5:15–17. How does this passage encourage you to embrace the end-in-mind lifestyle? Share together as many observations as you can from this passage.

5. Use your remaining small-group discussion time to share together the first pass of end goals you each wrote down in the "Before I die, I want to . . ." diagram in this chapter. After each person shares, ask for feedback. Use this feedback to help further clarify and think through the direction of your life.

Post-discussion Takeaways

Now that you have read this chapter and had your discussion time, what personal applications (new beliefs, priorities, behaviors, ways of thinking, etc.) will you leave with? Take a few minutes and record them in the space below.

Session 7
Discussion Questions

Chapter 10

Writing out your initial answers to these questions *before* your small-group meeting will enhance the quality of your discussions. Take a moment to record your answers.

1. Before this study how much reading and research had you put into building a reservoir of wisdom for understanding and successfully engaging a man? None? A little? A lot? Share your best piece of man wisdom with the group.

2. This chapter presents four fundamentals for successfully engaging a man. What impacted you the most in reading the section about what drives a man? Be specific.

3. What stood out to you after reading about the four top needs of a man? Are there any specific adjustments you could make right now to better address the needs of your man? Explain.

4. React to the three things you need to know and resolve before choosing a man. If married, did you know these three things about your husband before you were married? If so, how has that helped your relationship? If not, how did ignoring these things impact your marriage later on? Be specific.

5. As a married woman, knowing what you know now, what other things would you tell unmarried women are important to know and resolve before making a commitment to marriage? Tell why you think these things are so important.

6. What impacted you the most in reading the ten no-no's with a man? Explain. What is one immediate takeaway you can apply right now? Tell why.

7. Were any of these ten no-no's a surprise to you? Which one(s) and why? Are there any you have struggled with? Why?

8. What is the best piece of man wisdom you will take with you from this study and discussion? Explain.

Post-discussion Takeaways

Now that you have read this chapter and had your discussion time, what personal applications (new beliefs, priorities, behaviors, ways of thinking, etc.) will you leave with? Take a few minutes and record them in the space below.

Session 8
Discussion Questions

Chapter 11

Writing out your initial answers to these questions *before* your small-group meeting will enhance the quality of your discussions. Take a moment to record your answers.

1. What impacted you the most as you read the biblical outline for marriage on pages 166–67? What specifically appealed to you on that list? What did not? Explain.

2. What would have to change in your marriage for it to better align itself with the biblical outline on pages 166–67? What would be a good first step for you to move in that direction? Ask the group what advice they might have for you.

3. What specific responsibilities did your wedding vows charge you and your husband with in order to be married successfully? Explain. If you could rewrite your vows now, what would you want them to say? If you are single, what will you want your wedding vows to say?

4. Look at the biblical diagram for marriage that's on page 171. Do you see marriage this way? If not, what is the outline you are working from for your marriage (or future marriage)? Explain.

5. Share your thoughts about helper and head. Are you comfortable with these terms for your marriage or your future marriage? Why or why not?

6. What one or two things stand out to you from the research on marriage provided in chapter 11? Explain. As you observe couples around you, would you say their marriages confirm or challenge the findings of this research? Explain.

7. What is your greatest takeaway from this chapter? Explain.

Post-discussion Takeaways

Now that you have read this chapter and had your discussion time, what personal applications (new beliefs, priorities, behaviors, ways of thinking, etc.) will you leave with? Take a few minutes and record them in the space below.

Session 9
Discussion Questions

Chapter 12

Writing out your initial answers to these questions *before* your small-group meeting will enhance the quality of your discussions. Take a moment to record your answers.

1. Take time in this final session to review the previous eight discussions you have had together as a group. What has this New Eve study meant to you? What new insights do you believe you will leave with? Be specific.

2. In what ways has this study changed your perspective as a woman?

3. What practical applications from this study do you honestly think you will use?

4. In keeping with the story in chapter 12, what is your biggest challenge to becoming a New Eve?

5. What will be your first bold move?

6. How do you plan to work this bold move into your life? What will be your practical steps? How do you see this bold move changing the way you live life? Explain.

7. Conclude your New Eve study by praying for one another and the bold moves each woman intends to take.

Notes

Chapter 1

1.   Douglas B. Sosnik, Matthew J. Dowd, and Ron Fournier, *Applebee's America: How Successful Political, Business, and Religious Leaders Connect with the New American Community* (New York: Simon and Schuster, 2006), 224.

2.   Celinda Lake and Kellyanne Conway, *What Women Really Want: How American Women Are Quietly Erasing Political, Racial, Class, and Religious Lines to Change the Way We Live* (New York: Free Press, 2005), 2–3.

3.   Sylvia Ann Hewlett, *Creating a Life: Professional Women and the Quest for Children* (New York: Talk Miramax Books, 2002), 133.

4.   Peg Tyre and Daniel McGinn, "She Works, He Doesn't," *Newsweek*, 12 May 2003.

5.   Obtained from the Center for Women's Business Research, based on an analysis of data from the 2000 census.

6.   Tyre and McGinn, "She Works, He Doesn't." Also see Matt Krantz, "More Women Take CFO Roles," *USA Today*, 13 October 2004.

7.   See "Women Are the Backbone of the Christian Congregations in America," the Barna Group, 6 May 2000.

8.   Michelle Conlin, "The New Gender Gap: From Kindergarten to Grad School, Boys Are Becoming the Second Sex," *BusinessWeek*, 26 May 2003.

9.   "The Growing Gender Gaps in College Enrollment and Degree Attainment in the U.S. and Their Potential Economic and Social Consequences," a study prepared by the Center for Labor Market Studies at Northeastern University, May 2003.

10. Tamar Lewin, "At Colleges, Women Are Leaving Men in the Dust," *New York Times*, 9 July 2006.

11. "The Condition of Education," a 379-page report of federal statistics, June 1, 2006.

12. National Center for Education Statistics, http://nces.ed.gov/fastfacts/display.asp?id=72.

13. Mary Beth Marklein, "College Gender Gap Widens: 57% Are Women," *USA Today*, 19 October 2005.

14. Obtained from the Association to Advance Collegiate Schools of Business and *The Detroit News*, "Female MBA Students . . .," 29 July 2004.

15. "Full-Time Women MBA Students Outnumber Men for First Time at UNH," available from the University of New Hampshire's Media Relations Web site, 14 September 2005.

16. "Female Enrollment in U.S. Medical Schools," in *Modern Healthcare*, 24 May 2004.

17. Ted Gest, "Law Schools' New Female Face," in *U.S. News and World Report*, 9 April 2001.

18. Peg Tyre, "The Trouble with Boys," *Newsweek*, 30 January 2006.

19. Will Durant, *Caesar and Christ* (New York: MJF Books, 1944) is the source for most of the information on women's roles and rights in middle and late Rome. On the dramatic increase in divorce, sanctioned adultery, and abortion, see 134, 211, and 396. On the unpopularity of maternity, see 222. On women becoming doctors, lawyers, gladiators, and professionals of every sort, see 370.

20. Ibid., 438.

21. Simone de Beauvoir, quoted by Estelle Freedman in *No Turning Back: The History of Feminism and the Future of Women* (New York: Ballantine, 2002), 331.

22. Caitlin Flanagan, *To Hell with All That: Loving and Loathing Our Inner Housewife* (New York: Little, Brown, 2006), xvii.

23. Daniel Altiere, "Ubersexuals Leaving Metrosexuals at the Spa," http://www.foxnews.com, 24 October 2005.

24. Maria Shriver, *Ten Things I Wish I'd Known—Before I Went Out into the Real World* (New York: Warner, 2000), 61, 71.

25. Jeff Chu, "Ten Questions for Meredith Vieira," *Time*, 27 August 2006.

26. Joanne Kaufman, "Rachael Ray's Recipe for Joy," *Good Housekeeping*, August 2006.

27. Sylvia Ann Hewlett, *Creating a Life: Professional Women and the Quest for Children* (New York: Talk Miramax Books, 2002), 3.

28. Transcript, *Oprah*, 16 January 2002.

Chapter 2

1. David Kupelian, "The War on Father," 9 October 2006, WorldNetDaily, http://www.wnd.com/news/article.asp?ARTICLE_ID=52314 (accessed 3 January 2007).

2. Mary Ann B. Oakley, *Elizabeth Cady Stanton* (Old Westbury, NY: Feminist Press, 1972), 17.

3. Stanton, quoted by Estelle B. Freedman, *No Turning Back: The History of Feminism and the Future of Women* (New York: Ballantine, 2002), 17.

4. Jane Fonda, *My Life So Far* (New York: Random House, 2005), 496.

Chapter 3

1. Transcript, *Oprah*, 16 January 2002.

2. Carolyn Heilbrun, *Reinventing Womanhood* (New York: W. W. Norton, 1979), 196.

3. "She Works, He Doesn't," *Newsweek*, 12 May 2003. See also "Dad's Home Work Aids Cable's Career Women," Multichannel News, 21 July 2003.

4. Michelle Conlin, "Look Who's Bringing Home the Bacon," *BusinessWeek*, 27 January 2003.

5. The compromised position of males in contemporary society has become a popular subject in recent years, and female authors are among the most important voices raising the alarm. Susan Faludi, author of *Stiffed: The Betrayal of the American Male*, argues that men have been robbed of their sense of manhood by cultural confusion about such things as sex roles. In *The Trouble with Boys*, Angela Phillips explains how feminism has weakened manhood.

6. Linda Hirshman, "Unleashing the Wrath of Stay-at-Home Moms," *Washington Post*, sec. B-1, 18 June 2006.

7. Stephanie Coontz, *Marriage, a History: From Obedience to Intimacy, or How Love Conquered Marriage* (New York: Viking, 2005), 4.

8. David Brooks, *On Paradise Drive: How We Live Now (and Always Have) in the Future Tense* (New York: Simon and Schuster, 2004), 171.

9. Debra Rosenberg and Pat Wingert, "First Comes Junior in a Baby Carriage," *Newsweek*, 4 December 2006, 56.

10. Anne Kingston, *The Meaning of Wife: A Provocative Look at Women and Marriage in the Twenty-first Century* (New York: Farrar, Straus and Giroux, 2004), 1.

11. See also "Women Desire a Balance Between Career and Family," PRNewswire, 5 September 2000, which reported on a poll indicating that 62 percent of female respondents in California who work full-time would prefer to work part-time and from home.

12. "Census: More Women Childless Than Ever Before," *AP*, 25 October 2003.

13. Peter Drucker, "Managing Knowledge Means Managing Oneself," *Leader to Leader*, 16, Spring 2000.

14. Pamela Norris, *Eve: A Biography* (New York: New York University Press, 1999), 402.

Chapter 4

1. John Stott, *Decisive Issues Facing Christians Today* (Old Tappan, NJ: Revell, 1990), 120.

2.   George Barna, *The Future of the American Family* (Chicago: Moody Press, 1993), 121.

3.   Lisa Bergren and Rebecca Price, *What Women Want: The Life You Crave and How God Satisfies* (WaterBrook Press, 2007).

Chapter 5

1.   Michael Lemonick, "Everyone's Genealogical Mother," *Time*, 26 January 1987.

Chapter 6

1.   See *Men's Fraternity: The Quest for Authentic Manhood*, available from www.mensfraternity.com.

2.   Timothy George, "The Blessed Evangelical Mary," *Christianity Today*, December 2003.

3.   A. T. Robertson, *The Mother of Jesus: Her Problems and Her Glory* (Grand Rapids, MI: Baker, 1963), 13.

4.   Sylvia Ann Hewlett, *Creating a Life: Professional Women and the Quest for Children* (New York: Talk Mirimax Books, 2002), 42.

5.   Ibid., 4.

6.   Lisa Belkin, "The Opt-Out Revolution," *New York Times Magazine*, 26 October 2003.

7.   Barbara Bush's commencement address is available from the Wellesley Web site, http://www.wellesley.edu/PublicAffairs/Commencement/1990/bush.html.

8.   Danielle Crittenden, *What Our Mothers Didn't Tell Us* (New York: Touchstone, 1999), 183.

Chapter 7

1.   "Hooking Up, Hanging Out, and Hoping for Mr. Right: College Women on Mating and Dating Today. An Institute for American Values Report to the Independent Women's Forum," http://www.americanvalues.org/html/a-pr_hooking_up.html.

2.   Sylvia Ann Hewlett, *Creating a Life: Professional Women and the Quest for Children* (New York: Talk Mirimax Books, 2002), 89.

3.   Adapted from Hewlett, 301–2.

4.   www.brainyquote.com

5.   Stan Guthrie's interview with Brad Wilcox in *Christianity Today*, "What Married Women Want," October 2006, 122.

6.   "Hardwired to Connect." Purchasing information can be found online or from the Institute for American Values; 1841 Broadway, Suite 211; New York, NY 10023.

7.   From an NPR report by Vicky Que, 22 September 2003. The report can be accessed at http://www.npr.org/templates/story/story.php?storyId=1438731.

Chapter 8

1. Because they are doing missions work in a nation that officially bans Christianity and all varieties of missions work, the real names of this husband-and-wife team cannot be revealed out of concern for their safety.

2. Philippe Ariès, trans. Patricia M. Ranum, *Western Attitudes toward Death: From the Middle Ages to the Present* (Baltimore: Johns Hopkins University Press, 1974), 92.

3. National Center for Policy Analysis, November 2003, http://www.ncpa.org/pub/st/st264/.

4. Joan Didion, *The Year of Magical Thinking* (New York: Random House, 2005).

Chapter 9

1. Dr. Edward Diener, in Marilyn Elias, "Psychologists Know What Makes People Happy," *USA Today*, 10 December 2002. Dr. Diener is a psychologist at the University of Illinois.

2. Dr. William Sheldon, cited by Huston Smith, *Why Religion Matters: The Fate of the Human Spirit in an Age of Disbelief* (San Francisco: Harper SanFrancisco, 2001), 26.

3. Peter De Vries, *Let Me Count the Ways* (Boston: Little, Brown, 1965), 306–307.

4. Stephen Covey, *The Seven Habits of Highly Effective People* (New York: Simon and Schuster, 1989), 98.

5. David Brooks, *On Paradise Drive: How We Live Now (and Always Have) in the Future Tense* (New York: Simon and Schuster, 2004), 168.

6. Bob Buford, *Finishing Well: What People Who REALLY Live Do Differently* (Nashville: Integrity Publishers, 2004), xvii.

7. Linda Carroll, *Her Mother's Daughter: A Memoir of the Mother I Never Knew and of My Daughter, Courtney Love* (New York: Doubleday, 2005), 279.

8. The story of Blandina and the other Christian martyrs of Lyons is recounted by Eusebius Pamphilius, the bishop of Caesarea (b. AD 265), in his book *Ecclesiastical History*. See book 5, chapters 1–3. Remarkably, Eusebius's source is a letter that was written by the handful of Christians who remained in Lyons and the surrounding area after the persecution fires died down. The letter majestically begins as follows: "The servants of Christ dwelling at Lyons and Vienna, in Gaul, to those brethren in Asia and Phrygia, having the same faith and hope with us, peace and grace and glory from God the Father and Christ Jesus our Lord." A helpful summary with additional information is found in Kenneth Curtis and Daniel Graves, *Great Women in Christian History: 37 Women Who Changed Their World* (Camp Hill, PA: Christian Publications, 2004), 57.

9. This chart is adapted with author's permission from Bobb Biehl, *Focusing Your Life: A Proven Personal Retreat Guide Based on the "Life Blueprint Chart"* (Quick Wisdom Publishing, 2001), 135.

Chapter 10

1. Christopher Andersen, *The Day John Died* (New York: William Morrow, 2000), 32.
2. George Gilder, *Men and Marriage* (Gretna, LA: Pelican Publishing, 1993), 10.
3. Willard F. Harley Jr., *His Needs, Her Needs: Building an Affair-Proof Marriage* (Grand Rapids, MI: Revell, 1994), 77.
4. Will Durant, *Caesar and Christ* (New York: MJF Books, 1944), 370.
5. Harley, *His Needs, Her Needs,* 43–44.

Chapter 11

1. Steven L. Nock and W. Bradford Wilcox, "What's Love Got to Do with It? Equality, Equity, Commitment, and Women's Marital Quality," available in digital form from http://www.amazon.com. Other helpful information is found in Wilcox, *Soft Patriarchs, New Men: How Christianity Shapes Fathers and Husbands* (Chicago: University of Chicago Press, 2004).
2. "What Married Women Want," *Christianity Today,* October 2006.

Postscript

1. Carle C. Zimmerman, *Family and Civilization* (New York: Harper & Brothers, 1947), 801.
2. Stanley Kurtz, "Polygamy versus Democracy," *The Weekly Standard,* 5 June 2006.
3. Zimmerman, *Family and Civilization,* 810.
4. William Golding, *Lord of the Flies* (New York: Putnam, 1954), 40.

THE NEW MAN.

Robert Lewis Helps Men Discover and Apply
Biblical Principles to Authentic Manhood.

The *Men's Fraternity Bible* will be a valued resource to men worldwide. This gift boxed, pocket size edition features the complete text of the popular Holman CSB® translation plus nearly one-hundred pages of concise, stirring notes and biblical principles pulled from the Men's Fraternity ministry based upon the video teachings of pastor Robert Lewis. Available at bookstores everywhere.